SCRIPTURES TO
Live By

by
GREG MOHR

All Scripture quotations are taken from the King James
Version of the Bible.

ACKNOWLEDGEMENTS
SPECIAL THANKS TO:

Deborah Stalkup, Patsy Milligan, and Cammy Walters who spent many hours preparing the copy for print.

Kathy Gregg and Rebekah Gregg for their effort and encouragement to get this book republished.

My wife and best friend, Janice, who I cherish for her consistent encouragement, love, and support.

The Lord Jesus Christ, the author and finisher of my faith and this book.

SCRIPTURES TO LIVE BY

INTRODUCTION

When our second son, Michael, was fifteen months old each of his joints began to swell up twice their normal size. He also broke out in a strange rash and could no longer walk or crawl. Doctors diagnosed him with an untreatable muscular/arthritic condition they said if it continued to develop he would never walk again.

We had several people pray for him, including some healing evangelists, but his condition did not improve. Michael was crying all the time and seemed to be in constant pain. As my wife and I sought the Lord He led us to compile a list of several scriptures in three different categories: authority of the believer, the integrity of God's Word, and healing. He directed us to immerse ourselves in His Word by speaking these verses over Michael and to resist the enemy steadfastly with them on a daily basis.

After two months of meditating on these verses of scripture and speaking them over Michael and resisting the devil with them on a daily basis one passage of scripture from the list of seventy verses we had been speaking leapt off the page into our hearts. Those verses are Psalm 119:89-90, "Forever, O Lord, thy word is settled in heaven. Thy faithfulness is unto all generations…" This truth became alive in us that God's faithfulness to perform His Word includes Michael's generation!

Within a month after receiving this revelation Michael's condition began to improve. The swelling in his joints gradually went down. The rash was not as dominant as it once was. One month later he began to crawl again. Four months after this he began to walk. Six months later he was completely whole without any symptom of that dreaded disease. Praise be to God!

After this the Lord directed me to compile other categories of scripture that have the same power to effect change in our lives. That is the purpose for this book. I pray that as you read and meditate on each category of scripture in this book His Word will come alive to you, become life and health to all your flesh (Prov. 4:22), and bear fruit in every area of your life!

Wisdom, grace, and peace to you,

Greg Mohr

INDEX

SCRIPTURES TO LIVE BY

ANSWERED PRAYER

2 SAMUEL 22:7 – In my distress I called upon the LORD, and cried to my God: and he did hear my voice out of his temple, and my cry did enter into his ears.

2 CHRONICLES 7:14 – If my people, which are called by my name, shall humble themselves, and pray, and seek my face, and turn from their wicked ways; then will I hear from heaven, and will forgive their sin, and will heal their land.

2 CHRONICLES 16:9 – For the eyes of the LORD run to and fro throughout the whole earth, to shew himself strong in the behalf of them whose heart is perfect toward him.

PSALMS 4:3 - But know that the LORD hath set apart him that is godly for himself: the LORD will hear when I call unto him.

PSALMS 6:9 - The LORD hath heard my supplication; the LORD will receive my prayer.

PSALMS 9:12 - When he maketh inquisition for blood, he remembereth them: he forgetteth not the cry of the humble.

PSALMS 10:17 - LORD, thou hast heard the desire of the humble: thou wilt prepare their heart, thou wilt cause thine ear to hear:

PSALMS 17:6 - I have called upon thee, for thou wilt hear me, O God: incline thine ear unto me, and hear my speech.

PSALMS 18:6 - In my distress I called upon the LORD, and cried unto my God: he heard my voice out of his temple, and my cry came before him, even into his ears.

PSALMS 20:1 - The LORD hear thee in the day of trouble; the name of the God of Jacob defend thee;

PSALMS 20:5 - We will rejoice in thy salvation, and in the name of our God we will set up our banners: the LORD fulfil all thy petitions.

PSALMS 34:15 - The eyes of the LORD are upon the righteous, and his ears are open unto their cry.

PSALMS 37:4-5 - Delight thyself also in the LORD; and he shall give thee the desires of thine heart. Commit thy way unto the LORD; trust also in him; and he shall bring it to pass.

PSALMS 40:1 - I waited patiently for the LORD; and he inclined unto me, and heard my cry.

PSALMS 46:1 - God is our refuge and strength, a very present help in trouble.

PSALMS 50:14-15 - Offer unto God thanksgiving; and pay thy vows unto the most High: And call upon me in the day of trouble: I will deliver thee, and thou shalt glorify me.

PSALMS 65:2 - O thou that hearest prayer, unto thee shall all flesh come.

PSALMS 66:18-20 - If I regard iniquity in my heart, the Lord will not hear me: But verily God hath heard me; he hath attended to the voice of my prayer. Blessed be God, which hath not turned away my prayer, nor his mercy from me.

PSALMS 81:7 - Thou calledst in trouble, and I delivered thee; I answered thee in the secret place of thunder: I proved thee at the waters of Meribah. Selah.

PSALMS 86:5-7 - For thou, Lord, art good, and ready to forgive; and plenteous in mercy unto all them that call upon thee. Give ear, O LORD, unto my prayer; and attend to the voice of my supplications. In the day of my trouble I will call upon thee: for thou wilt answer me.

PSALMS 91:14-16 - Because he hath set his love upon me, therefore will I deliver him: I will set him on high, because he hath known my name. He shall call upon me, and I will answer him: I will be with him in trouble; I will deliver him, and honour him. With long life will I satisfy him, and show him my salvation.

PSALMS 102:17 - He will regard the prayer of the destitute, and not despise their prayer.

PSALMS 138:3 - In the day when I cried thou answeredst me, and strengthenedst me with strength in my soul.

PSALMS 145:16 - Thou openest thine hand, and satisfiest the desire of every living thing.

PSALMS 145:18-19 - The LORD is nigh unto all them that call upon him, to all that call upon him in truth. He will fulfil the desire of them that fear him: he also will hear their cry, and will save them.

PROVERBS 10:24 - The fear of the wicked, it shall come upon him: but the desire of the righteous shall be granted.

PROVERBS 15:29 - The LORD is far from the wicked: but he heareth the prayer of the righteous.

ISAIAH 41:21 - Produce your cause, saith the LORD; bring forth your strong reasons, saith the King of Jacob.

ISAIAH 43:26 - Put me in remembrance: let us plead together: declare thou, that thou mayest be justified.

ISAIAH 45:11 - Thus saith the LORD, the Holy One of Israel, and his Maker, Ask me of things to come concerning my sons, and concerning the work of my hands command ye me.

ISAIAH 59:1 - Behold, the LORD'S hand is not shortened, that it cannot save; neither his ear heavy, that it cannot hear:

JEREMIAH 29:12-13 - Then shall ye call upon me, and ye shall go and pray unto me, and I will hearken unto you. And ye shall seek me, and find me, when ye shall search for me with all your heart.

JEREMIAH 33:3 - Call unto me, and I will answer thee, and show thee great and mighty things, which thou knowest not.

MATTHEW 7:7-8 - Ask, and it shall be given you; seek, and ye shall find; knock, and it shall be opened unto you: For every one that asketh receiveth; and he that seeketh findeth; and to him that knocketh it shall be opened.

MATTHEW 7:11 - If ye then, being evil, know how to give good gifts unto your children, how much more shall your Father which is in heaven give good things to them that ask him?

MATTHEW 18:19-20 - Again I say unto you, That if two of you shall agree on earth as touching any thing that they shall ask, it shall be done for them of my Father which is in heaven. For where two or three are gathered together in my name, there am I in the midst of them.

MATTHEW 21:22 - And all things, whatsoever ye shall ask in prayer, believing, ye shall receive.

MARK 11:24 - Therefore I say unto you, What things soever ye desire, when ye pray, believe that ye receive them, and ye shall have them.

JOHN 14:13-14 - And whatsoever ye shall ask in my name, that will I do, that the Father may be glorified in the Son. If ye shall ask any thing in my name, I will do it.

JOHN 15:7 - If ye abide in me, and my words abide in you, ye shall ask what ye will, and it shall be done unto you.

JOHN 15:16 - Ye have not chosen me, but I have chosen you, and ordained you, that ye should go and bring forth fruit, and that your fruit should remain: that whatsoever ye shall ask of the Father in my name, he may give it you.

JOHN 16:23-24 - And in that day ye shall ask me nothing. Verily, verily, I say unto you, Whatsoever ye shall ask the Father in my name, he will give it you. Hitherto have ye asked nothing in my name: ask, and ye shall receive, that your joy may be full.

EPHESIANS 3:20-21 - Now unto him that is able to do exceeding abundantly above all that we ask or think, according to the power that worketh in us, Unto him be glory in the church by Christ Jesus throughout all ages, world without end. Amen.

PHILIPPIANS 4:6 - Be careful for nothing; but in every thing by prayer and supplication with thanksgiving let your requests be made known unto God.

JAMES 4:2-3 - Ye lust, and have not: ye kill, and desire to have, and cannot obtain: ye fight and war, yet ye have not, because ye ask not. Ye ask, and receive not, because ye ask amiss, that ye may consume it upon your lusts.

JAMES 5:16 - Confess your faults one to another, and pray one for another, that ye may be healed. The effectual fervent prayer of a righteous man availeth much.

1 PETER 3:12 - For the eyes of the Lord are over the righteous, and his ears are open unto their prayers: but the face of the Lord is against them that do evil.

2 PETER 1:3-4 - According as his divine power hath given unto us all things that pertain unto life and godliness, through the knowledge of him that hath called us to glory and virtue: Whereby are given unto us exceeding great and precious promises: that by these ye might be partakers of the divine nature, having escaped the corruption that is in the world through lust.

1 JOHN 3:21-22 - Beloved, if our heart condemn us not, then have we confidence toward God. And whatsoever we ask, we receive of him, because we keep his commandments, and do those things that are pleasing in his sight.

1 JOHN 5:14-15 - And this is the confidence that we have in him, that, if we ask any thing according to his will, he heareth us: And if we know that he hear us, whatsoever we ask, we know that we have the petitions that we desired of him.

SCRIPTURES TO LIVE BY

ANXIETY

PSALMS 4:8 - I will both lay me down in peace, and sleep: for thou, LORD, only makest me dwell in safety.

PSALMS 55:22 - Cast thy burden upon the LORD, and he shall sustain thee: he shall never suffer the righteous to be moved.

PSALMS 119:165 - Great peace have they which love thy law: and nothing shall offend them.

PROVERBS 16:3 - Commit thy works unto the LORD, and thy thoughts shall be established.

ISAIAH 26:3 - Thou wilt keep him in perfect peace, whose mind is stayed on thee: because he trusteth in thee.

ISAIAH 41:10 - Fear thou not; for I am with thee: be not dismayed; for I am thy God: I will strengthen thee; yea, I will help thee; yea, I will uphold thee with the right hand of my righteousness.

MATTHEW 6:25-34 - Therefore I say unto you, Take no thought for your life, what ye shall eat, or what ye shall drink; nor yet for your body, what ye shall put on. Is not the life more than meat, and the body than raiment? Behold the fowls of the air: for they sow not, neither do they reap, nor gather into barns; yet your heavenly Father feedeth them. Are ye not much better than they? Which of you by taking thought can add one cubit unto his stature? And why take ye thought for raiment? Consider the lilies of the field, how they grow; they toil not, neither do they spin: And yet I say unto you, That even Solomon in all his glory was not arrayed like one of these. Wherefore, if God so clothe the grass of the field, which to day is, and to morrow is cast into the oven, shall he not much more clothe you, O ye of little faith? Therefore take no thought, saying, What shall we eat? or, What shall we drink? or, Wherewithal shall we be clothed? (For after all these things do the Gentiles seek:) for your heavenly Father knoweth that ye have need of all these things. But seek ye first the kingdom of God, and his righteousness; and all these things shall be added unto you. Take therefore no thought for the morrow: for the morrow shall take thought for the things of itself. Sufficient unto the day is the evil thereof.

MARK 4:18-19 - And these are they which are sown among thorns; such as hear the word, And the cares of this world, and the deceitfulness of riches, and the lusts of other things entering in, choke the word, and it becometh unfruitful.

LUKE 21:34 - And take heed to yourselves, lest at any time your hearts be overcharged with surfeiting, and drunkenness, and cares of this life, and so that day come upon you unawares.

LUKE 21:36 - Watch ye therefore, and pray always, that ye may be accounted worthy to escape all these things that shall come to pass, and to stand before the Son of man.

JOHN 14:1 - Let not your heart be troubled: ye believe in God, believe also in me.

JOHN 14:27 - Peace I leave with you, my peace I give unto you: not as the world giveth, give I unto you. Let not your heart be troubled, neither let it be afraid.

JOHN 16:33 - These things I have spoken unto you, that in me ye might have peace. In the world ye shall have tribulation: but be of good cheer; I have overcome the world.

ROMANS 8:6 - For to be carnally minded is death; but to be spiritually minded is life and peace.

PHILIPPIANS 4:4-8 - Rejoice in the Lord alway: and again I say, Rejoice. Let your moderation be known unto all men. The Lord is at hand. Be careful for nothing; but in every thing by prayer and supplication with thanksgiving let your requests be made known unto God. And the peace of God, which passeth all understanding, shall keep your hearts and minds through Christ Jesus. Finally, brethren, whatsoever things are true, whatsoever things are honest, whatsoever things are just, whatsoever things are pure, whatsoever things are lovely, whatsoever things are of good report; if there be any virtue, and if there be any praise, think on these things.

HEBREWS 13:5 - Let your conversation be without covetousness; and be content with such things as ye have: for he hath said, I will never leave thee, nor forsake thee.

1 PETER 5:6-7 - Humble yourselves therefore under the mighty hand of God, that he may exalt you in due time: Casting all your care upon him; for he careth for you.

AUTHORITY

DEUTERONOMY 28:13 - And the LORD shall make thee the head, and not the tail; and thou shalt be above only, and thou shalt not be beneath; if that thou hearken unto the commandments of the LORD thy God, which I command thee this day, to observe and to do them:

DEUTERONOMY 32:30 - How should one chase a thousand, and two put ten thousand to flight, except their Rock had sold them, and the LORD had shut them up?

JOSHUA 1:5 - There shall not any man be able to stand before thee all the days of thy life: as I was with Moses, so I will be with thee: I will not fail thee, nor forsake thee.

JOSHUA 23:9-10 - One man of you shall chase a thousand: for the LORD your God, he it is that fighteth for you, as he hath promised you.

PSALMS 8:2 - Out of the mouth of babes and sucklings hast thou ordained strength because of thine enemies, that thou mightest still the enemy and the avenger.

PSALMS 44:5 - Through thee will we push down our enemies: through thy name will we tread them under that rise up against us.

PSALMS 47:3 - He shall subdue the people under us, and the nations under our feet.

PSALMS 66:3 - Say unto God, How terrible art thou in thy works! through the greatness of thy power shall thine enemies submit themselves unto thee.

PSALMS 68:1 - Let God arise, let his enemies be scattered: let them also that hate him flee before him.

PSALMS 91:13 - Thou shalt tread upon the lion and adder: the young lion and the dragon shalt thou trample under feet.

ISAIAH 10:27 - And it shall come to pass in that day, that his burden shall be taken away from off thy shoulder, and his yoke from off thy neck, and the yoke shall be destroyed because of the anointing.

ISAIAH 54:17 - No weapon that is formed against thee shall prosper; and every tongue that shall rise against thee in judgment thou shalt condemn. This is the heritage of the servants of the LORD, and their righteousness is of me, saith the LORD.

ISAIAH 58:6 - Is not this the fast that I have chosen? to loose the bands of wickedness, to undo the heavy burdens, and to let the oppressed go free, and that ye break every yoke?

ISAIAH 59:19 - So shall they fear the name of the LORD from the west, and his glory from the rising of the sun. When the enemy shall come in like a flood, the Spirit of the LORD shall lift up a standard against him.

MARK 16:17 - And these signs shall follow them that believe; In my name shall they cast out devils; they shall speak with new tongues;

LUKE 9:1 - Then he called his twelve disciples together, and gave them power and authority over all devils, and to cure diseases.

LUKE 10:19 - Behold, I give unto you power to tread on serpents and scorpions, and over all the power of the enemy: and nothing shall by any means hurt you.

ACTS 19:20 - So mightily grew the word of God and prevailed.

ACTS 26:18 - To open their eyes, and to turn them from darkness to light, and from the power of Satan unto God, that they may receive forgiveness of sins, and inheritance among them which are sanctified by faith that is in me.

ROMANS 6:14 - For sin shall not have dominion over you: for ye are not under the law, but under grace.

ROMANS 8:2 - For the law of the Spirit of life in Christ Jesus hath made me free from the law of sin and death.

ROMANS 8:31 - What shall we then say to these things? If God be for us, who can be against us?

2 CORINTHIANS 10:4-5 - For the weapons of our warfare are not carnal, but mighty through God to the pulling down of strong holds;) Casting down imaginations, and every high thing that exalteth itself against the knowledge of God, and bringing into captivity every thought to the obedience of Christ;

EPHESIANS 1:19-20 - And what is the exceeding greatness of his power to us-ward who believe, according to the working of his mighty power, Which he wrought in Christ, when he raised him from the dead, and set him at his own right hand in the heavenly places,

EPHESIANS 4:27 - Neither give place to the devil.

EPHESIANS 6:10-18 - Finally, my brethren, be strong in the Lord, and in the power of his might. Put on the whole armour of God, that ye may be able to stand against the wiles of the devil. For we wrestle not against flesh and blood, but against principalities, against powers, against the rulers of the darkness of this world, against spiritual wickedness in high places. Wherefore take unto you the whole armour of God, that ye may be able to withstand in the evil day, and having done all, to stand. Stand therefore, having your loins girt about with truth, and having on the breastplate of righteousness; And your feet shod with the preparation of the gospel of peace; Above all, taking the shield of faith, wherewith ye shall be able to quench all the fiery darts of the wicked. And take the helmet of salvation, and the sword of the Spirit, which is the word of God: Praying always with all prayer and supplication in the Spirit, and watching thereunto with all perseverance and supplication for all saints;

PHILIPPIANS 1:28 - And in nothing terrified by your adversaries: which is to them an evident token of perdition, but to you of salvation, and that of God.

PHILIPPIANS 2:9-10 - Wherefore God also hath highly exalted him, and given him a name which is above every name: That at the name of Jesus every knee should bow, of things in heaven, and things in earth, and things under the earth;

COLOSSIANS 1:13 - Who hath delivered us from the power of darkness, and hath translated us into the kingdom of his dear Son:

COLOSSIANS 2:15 - And having spoiled principalities and powers, he made a show of them openly, triumphing over them in it.

HEBREWS 2:14-15 - Forasmuch then as the children are partakers of flesh and blood, he also himself likewise took part of the same; that through death he might destroy him that had the power of death, that is, the devil; And deliver them who through fear of death were all their lifetime subject to bondage.

JAMES 4:7 - Submit yourselves therefore to God. Resist the devil, and he will flee from you.

1 PETER 4:1 - Forasmuch then as Christ hath suffered for us in the flesh, arm yourselves likewise with the same mind: for he that hath suffered in the flesh hath ceased from sin;

1 PETER 5:8-9 - Be sober, be vigilant; because your adversary the devil, as a roaring lion, walketh about, seeking whom he may devour: Whom resist stedfast in the faith, knowing that the same afflictions are accomplished in your brethren that are in the world.

1 JOHN 3:8 - He that committeth sin is of the devil; for the devil sinneth from the beginning. For this purpose the Son of God was manifested, that he might destroy the works of the devil.

1 JOHN 5:18 - We know that whosoever is born of God sinneth not; but he that is begotten of God keepeth himself, and that wicked one toucheth him not.

REVELATION 12:11 - And they overcame him by the blood of the Lamb, and by the word of their testimony; and they loved not their lives unto the death.

BOLDNESS

PROVERBS 28:1 - The wicked flee when no man pursueth: but the righteous are bold as a lion.

ECCLESIASTES 8:1 - Who is as the wise man? and who knoweth the interpretation of a thing? a man's wisdom maketh his face to shine, and the boldness of his face shall be changed.

JOHN 7:26 - But, lo, he speaketh boldly, and they say nothing unto him. Do the rulers know indeed that this is the very Christ?

ACTS 4:13 - Now when they saw the boldness of Peter and John, and perceived that they were unlearned and ignorant men, they marvelled; and they took knowledge of them, that they had been with Jesus.

ACTS 4:29-31 - And now, Lord, behold their threatenings: and grant unto thy servants, that with all boldness they may speak thy word, By stretching forth thine hand to heal; and that signs and wonders may be done by the name of thy holy child Jesus. And when they had prayed, the place was shaken where they were assembled together; and they were all filled with the Holy Ghost, and they spake the word of God with boldness.

ACTS 9:29 - And he (Saul) spake boldly in the name of the Lord Jesus, and disputed against the Grecians: but they went about to slay him.

ACTS 13:46 - Then Paul and Barnabas waxed bold, and said, It was necessary that the word of God should first have been spoken to you: but seeing ye put it from you, and judge yourselves unworthy of everlasting life, lo, we turn to the Gentiles.

EPHESIANS 3:12 - In whom we have boldness and access with confidence by the faith of him.

EPHESIANS 6:19-20 - And for me, that utterance may be given unto me, that I may open my mouth boldly, to make known the mystery of the gospel, For which I am an ambassador in bonds: that therein I may speak boldly, as I ought to speak.

PHILIPPIANS 1:14 - And many of the brethren in the Lord, waxing confident by my bonds, are much more bold to speak the word without fear.

PHILIPPIANS 1:20 - According to my earnest expectation and my hope, that in nothing I shall be ashamed, but that with all boldness, as always, so now also Christ shall be magnified in my body, whether it be by life, or by death.

1 THESSALONIANS 2:2 - But even after that we had suffered before, and were shamefully entreated, as ye know, at Philippi, we were bold in our God to speak unto you the gospel of God with much contention.

HEBREWS 4:16 - Let us therefore come boldly unto the throne of grace, that we may obtain mercy, and find grace to help in time of need.

HEBREWS 10:19 - Having therefore, brethren, boldness to enter into the holiest by the blood of Jesus,

1 JOHN 2:28 - And now, little children, abide in him; that, when he shall appear, we may have confidence, and not be ashamed before him at his coming.

1 JOHN 4:17 - Herein is our love made perfect, that we may have boldness in the day of judgment: because as he is, so are we in this world.

SCRIPTURES TO LIVE BY

CHILDBEARING
(CONCEPTION)

GENESIS 1:27-28 - So God created man in his own image, in the image of God created he him; male and female created he them. And God blessed them, and God said unto them, Be fruitful, and multiply, and replenish the earth, and subdue it: and have dominion over the fish of the sea, and over the fowl of the air, and over every living thing that moveth upon the earth.

GENESIS 25:21 - And Isaac entreated the LORD for his wife, because she was barren: and the LORD was entreated of him, and Rebekah his wife conceived.

EXODUS 23:26 - There shall nothing cast their young, nor be barren, in thy land: the number of thy days I will fulfil.

DEUTERONOMY 7:14 - Thou shalt be blessed above all people: there shall not be male or female barren among you, or among your cattle.

JUDGES 13:3 – And the angel of the LORD appeared unto the woman, and said unto her, Behold now, thou art barren, and bearest not: but thou shalt conceive, and bear a son.

1 SAMUEL 1:30 – Wherefore it came to pass, when the time was come about after Hannah had conceived, that she bare a son, and called his name Samuel, saying, Because I have asked him of the LORD.

PSALMS 113:9 - He maketh the barren woman to keep house, and to be a joyful mother of children. Praise ye the LORD.

PSALMS 128:3 - Thy wife shall be as a fruitful vine by the sides of thine house: thy children like olive plants round about thy table.

LUKE 1:13,24-25 - But the angel said unto him, Fear not, Zacharias: for thy prayer is heard; and thy wife Elisabeth shall bear thee a son, and thou shalt call his name John. And after those days his wife Elisabeth conceived, and hid herself five months, saying, Thus hath the Lord dealt with me in the days wherein he looked on me, to take away my reproach among men.

ROMANS 2:11 - For there is no respect of persons with God.

GALATIANS 4:27 - For it is written, Rejoice, thou barren that bearest not; break forth and cry, thou that travailest not: for the desolate hath many more children than she which hath an husband.

HEBREWS 11:11 - Through faith also Sara herself received strength to conceive seed, and was delivered of a child when she was past age, because she judged him faithful who had promised.

CHILDBEARING
(DELIVERY)

GENESIS 49:25 - Even by the God of thy father, who shall help thee; and by the Almighty, who shall bless thee with blessings of heaven above, blessings of the deep that lieth under, blessings of the breasts, and of the womb:

EXODUS 23:26 - There shall nothing cast their young, nor be barren, in thy land: the number of thy days I will fulfil.

DEUTERONOMY 28:4 - Blessed shall be the fruit of thy body, and the fruit of thy ground, and the fruit of thy cattle, the increase of thy kine, and the flocks of thy sheep.

DEUTERONOMY 31:6 - Be strong and of a good courage, fear not, nor be afraid of them: for the LORD thy God, he it is that doth go with thee; he will not fail thee, nor forsake thee.

PSALMS 22:9-10 - But thou art he that took me out of the womb: thou didst make me hope when I was upon my mother's breasts. I was cast upon thee from the womb: thou art my God from my mother's belly.

PSALMS 91:11 - For he shall give his angels charge over thee, to keep thee in all thy ways.

PSALMS 127:3 - Lo, children are an heritage of the LORD: and the fruit of the womb is his reward.

ISAIAH 40:11 - He shall feed his flock like a shepherd: he shall gather the lambs with his arm, and carry them in his bosom, and shall gently lead those that are with young.

ISAIAH 44:3 - For I will pour water upon him that is thirsty, and floods upon the dry ground: I will pour my spirit upon thy seed, and my blessing upon thine offspring:

ISAIAH 53:4 - Surely he hath borne our griefs, and carried our sorrows: yet we did esteem him stricken, smitten of God, and afflicted.

ISAIAH 66:7 - Before she travailed, she brought forth; before her pain came, she was delivered of a man child.

ISAIAH 66:9 - Shall I bring to the birth, and not cause to bring forth? saith the LORD: shall I cause to bring forth, and shut the womb? saith thy God.

ISAIAH 65:23 - They shall not labour in vain, nor bring forth for trouble; for they are the seed of the blessed of the LORD, and their offspring with them.

JEREMIAH 32:27 - Behold, I am the LORD, the God of all flesh: is there any thing too hard for me?

GENESIS 3:16, GALATIANS 3:13 - Unto the woman he said, I will greatly multiply thy sorrow and thy conception; in sorrow thou shalt bring forth children; and thy desire shall be to thy husband, and he shall rule over thee. Christ hath redeemed us from the curse of the law, being made a curse for us: for it is written, Cursed is every one that hangeth on a tree:

1 TIMOTHY 2:15 - Notwithstanding she shall be saved in childbearing, if they continue in faith and charity and holiness with sobriety.

PHILIPPIANS 1:6 - Being confident of this very thing, that he which hath begun a good work in you will perform it until the day of Jesus Christ:

2 TIMOTHY 1:7 - For God hath not given us the spirit of fear; but of power, and of love, and of a sound mind.

SCRIPTURES TO LIVE BY

CHILD TRAINING

GENESIS 18:19 - For I know him, that he will command his children and his household after him, and they shall keep the way of the LORD, to do justice and judgment; that the LORD may bring upon Abraham that which he hath spoken of him.

DEUTERONOMY 4:9 - Only take heed to thyself, and keep thy soul diligently, lest thou forget the things which thine eyes have seen, and lest they depart from thy heart all the days of thy life: but teach them thy sons, and thy sons' sons;

DEUTERONOMY 6:6-9 - And these words, which I command thee this day, shall be in thine heart: And thou shalt teach them diligently unto thy children, and shalt talk of them when thou sittest in thine house, and when thou walkest by the way, and when thou liest down, and when thou risest up. And thou shalt bind them for a sign upon thine hand, and they shall be as frontlets between thine eyes. And thou shalt write them upon the posts of thy house, and on thy gates.

DEUTERONOMY 11:18-21 – Therefore shall ye lay up these my words in your heart and in your soul, and bind them for a sign upon your hand, that they may be as frontlets between your eyes. And ye shall teach them your children, speaking of them when thou sittest in thine house, and when thou walkest by the way, when thou liest down, and when thou risest up. And thou shalt write them upon the door posts of thine house, and upon thy gates: That your days may be multiplies, and the days of your children, in the land which the LORD sware unto your fathers to give them, as the days of heaven upon the earth.

DEUTERONOMY 28:2-4 - And all these blessings shall come on thee, and overtake thee, if thou shalt hearken unto the voice of the LORD thy God. Blessed shalt thou be in the city, and blessed shalt thou be in the field. Blessed shall be the fruit of thy body, and the fruit of thy ground, and the fruit of thy cattle, the increase of thy kine, and the flocks of thy sheep.

DEUTERONOMY 29:29 - The secret things belong unto the LORD our God: but those things which are revealed belong unto us and to our children for ever, that we may do all the words of this law.

JUDGES 13:24 - And the woman bare a son, and called his name Samson: and the child grew, and the LORD blessed him.

PSALMS 78:5-7 - For he established a testimony in Jacob, and appointed a law in Israel, which he commanded our fathers, that they should make them known to their children: That the generation to come might know them, even the children which should be born; who should arise and declare them to their children: That they might set their hope in God, and not forget the works of God, but keep his commandments:

PROVERBS 13:24 - He that spareth his rod hateth his son: but he that loveth him chasteneth him betimes.

PROVERBS 19:18 - Chasten thy son while there is hope, and let not thy soul spare for his crying.

PROVERBS 20:11 - Even a child is known by his doings, whether his work be pure, and whether it be right.

PROVERBS 20:30 - The blueness of a wound cleanseth away evil: so do stripes the inward parts of the belly.

PROVERBS 22:6 - Train up a child in the way he should go: and when he is old, he will not depart from it.

PROVERBS 22:15 - Foolishness is bound in the heart of a child; but the rod of correction shall drive it far from him.

PROVERBS 23:13-14 - Withhold not correction from the child: for if thou beatest him with the rod, he shall not die. Thou shalt beat him with the rod, and shalt deliver his soul from hell.

PROVERBS 29:15 - The rod and reproof give wisdom: but a child left to himself bringeth his mother to shame.

ISAIAH 54:13 - And all thy children shall be taught of the LORD; and great shall be the peace of thy children.

LUKE 2:40 - And the child grew, and waxed strong in spirit, filled with wisdom: and the grace of God was upon him.

LUKE 2:51-52 - And he went down with them, and came to Nazareth, and was subject unto them: but his mother kept all these sayings in her heart. And Jesus increased in wisdom and stature, and in favour with God and man.

1 CORINTHIANS 15:33:34 - Be not deceived: evil communications corrupt good manners. Awake to righteousness, and sin not; for some have not the knowledge of God: I speak this to your shame.

EPHESIANS 6:1-4 - Children, obey your parents in the Lord: for this is right. Honour thy father and mother; which is the first commandment with promise; That it may be well with thee, and thou mayest live long on the earth. And, ye fathers, provoke not your children to wrath: but bring them up in the nurture and admonition of the Lord.

COLOSSIANS 3:20-21 - Children, obey your parents in all things: for this is well pleasing unto the Lord. Fathers, provoke not your children to anger, lest they be discouraged.

DELIVERANCE

PSALMS 17:13 - Arise, O LORD, disappoint him, cast him down: deliver my soul from the wicked, which is thy sword:

PSALMS 18:2 - The LORD is my rock, and my fortress, and my deliverer; my God, my strength, in whom I will trust; my buckler, and the horn of my salvation, and my high tower.

PSALMS 18:19 - He brought me forth also into a large place; he delivered me, because he delighted in me.

PSALMS 33:18-19 - Behold, the eye of the LORD is upon them that fear him, upon them that hope in his mercy; To deliver their soul from death, and to keep them alive in famine.

PSALMS 34:7 - The angel of the LORD encampeth round about them that fear him, and delivereth them.

PSALMS 34:19 - Many are the afflictions of the righteous: but the LORD delivereth him out of them all.

PSALMS 56:13 - For thou hast delivered my soul from death: wilt not thou deliver my feet from falling, that I may walk before God in the light of the living?

PSALMS 91:3 - Surely he shall deliver thee from the snare of the fowler, and from the noisome pestilence.

PSALMS 91:14 - Because he hath set his love upon me, therefore will I deliver him: I will set him on high, because he hath known my name.

PSALMS 94:12-13 - Blessed is the man whom thou chastenest, O LORD, and teachest him out of thy law; That thou mayest give him rest from the days of adversity, until the pit be digged for the wicked.

PSALMS 97:10 - Ye that love the LORD, hate evil: he preserveth the souls of his saints; he delivereth them out of the hand of the wicked.

PSALMS 102:19-20 - For he hath looked down from the height of his sanctuary; from heaven did the LORD behold the earth; To hear the groaning of the prisoner; to loose those that are appointed to death;

PSALMS 107:20 - He sent his word, and healed them, and delivered them from their destructions.

PSALMS 116:8 - For thou hast delivered my soul from death, mine eyes from tears, and my feet from falling.

PSALMS 119:134 - Deliver me from the oppression of man: so will I keep thy precepts.

PSALMS 119:170 - Let my supplication come before thee: deliver me according to thy word.

PSALMS 146:7 - Which executeth judgment for the oppressed: which giveth food to the hungry. The LORD looseth the prisoners:

PROVERBS 10:2 - Treasures of wickedness profit nothing: but righteousness delivereth from death.

PROVERBS 11:6 - The righteousness of the upright shall deliver them: but transgressors shall be taken in their own naughtiness.

PROVERBS 11:9 - An hypocrite with his mouth destroyeth his neighbour: but through knowledge shall the just be delivered.

PROVERBS 11:21 - Though hand join in hand, the wicked shall not be unpunished: but the seed of the righteous shall be delivered.

PROVERBS 12:6 - The words of the wicked are to lie in wait for blood: but the mouth of the upright shall deliver them.

PROVERBS 28:26 - He that trusteth in his own heart is a fool: but whoso walketh wisely, he shall be delivered.

ISAIAH 10:27 - And it shall come to pass in that day, that his burden shall be taken away from off thy shoulder, and his yoke from off thy neck, and the yoke shall be destroyed because of the anointing.

ISAIAH 58:6 - Is not this the fast that I have chosen? to loose the bands of wickedness, to undo the heavy burdens, and to let the oppressed go free, and that ye break every yoke?

2 SAMUEL 22:2-3 - And he said, The LORD is my rock, and my fortress, and my deliverer; The God of my rock; in him will I trust: he is my shield, and the horn of my salvation, my high tower, and my refuge, my saviour; thou savest me from violence.

NEHEMIAH 9:28 - But after they had rest, they did evil again before thee: therefore leftest thou them in the hand of their enemies, so that they had the dominion over them: yet when they returned, and cried unto thee, thou heardest them from heaven; and many times didst thou deliver them according to thy mercies;

JOB 33:28 - He will deliver his soul from going into the pit, and his life shall see the light.

JOB 36:15 - He delivereth the poor in his affliction, and openeth their ears in oppression.

JEREMIAH 1:8 - Be not afraid of their faces: for I am with thee to deliver thee, saith the LORD.

JEREMIAH 1:19 - And they shall fight against thee; but they shall not prevail against thee; for I am with thee, saith the LORD, to deliver thee.

JEREMIAH 15:21 - And I will deliver thee out of the hand of the wicked, and I will redeem thee out of the hand of the terrible.

JEREMIAH 39:17-18 - But I will deliver thee in that day, saith the LORD: and thou shalt not be given into the hand of the men of whom thou art afraid. For I will surely deliver thee, and thou shalt not fall by the sword, but thy life shall be for a prey unto thee: because thou hast put thy trust in me, saith the LORD.

DANIEL 6:27 - He delivereth and rescueth, and he worketh signs and wonders in heaven and in earth, who hath delivered Daniel from the power of the lions.

MATTHEW 16:19 - And I will give unto thee the keys of the kingdom of heaven: and whatsoever thou shalt bind on earth shall be bound in heaven: and whatsoever thou shalt loose on earth shall be loosed in heaven.

LUKE 4:18 - The Spirit of the Lord is upon me, because he hath anointed me to preach the gospel to the poor; he hath sent me to heal the brokenhearted, to preach deliverance to the captives, and recovering of sight to the blind, to set at liberty them that are bruised,

LUKE 11:4 - And forgive us our sins; for we also forgive every one that is indebted to us. And lead us not into temptation; but deliver us from evil.

LUKE 13:16 - And ought not this woman, being a daughter of Abraham, whom Satan hath bound, lo, these eighteen years, be loosed from this bond on the sabbath day?

JOHN 8:31-32 - Then said Jesus to those Jews which believed on him, If ye continue in my word, then are ye my disciples indeed; And ye shall know the truth, and the truth shall make you free.

ACTS 26:16-18 - But rise, and stand upon thy feet: for I have appeared unto thee for this purpose, to make thee a minister and a witness both of these things which thou hast seen, and of those things in the which I will appear unto thee; Delivering thee from the people, and from the Gentiles, unto whom now I send thee, To open their eyes, and to turn them from darkness to light, and from the power of Satan unto God, that they may receive forgiveness of sins, and inheritance among them which are sanctified by faith that is in me.

ROMANS 8:2 - For the law of the Spirit of life in Christ Jesus hath made me free from the law of sin and death.

2 CORINTHIANS 1:10 - Who delivered us from so great a death, and doth deliver: in whom we trust that he will yet deliver us;

GALATIANS 1:3-4 – Grace be to you and peace from God the Father, and from our Lord Jesus Christ, Who gave himself for our sins, that he might deliver us from this present evil world, according to the will of God and our Father:

GALATIANS 5:1 - Stand fast therefore in the liberty wherewith Christ hath made us free, and be not entangled again with the yoke of bondage.

COLOSSIANS 1:12-13 - Giving thanks unto the Father, which hath made us meet to be partakers of the inheritance of the saints in light: Who hath delivered us from the power of darkness, and hath translated us into the kingdom of his dear Son:

2 THESSALONIANS 3:2 - And that we may be delivered from unreasonable and wicked men: for all men have not faith.

2 TIMOTHY 4:18 - And the Lord shall deliver me from every evil work, and will preserve me unto his heavenly kingdom: to whom be glory for ever and ever. Amen.

HEBREWS 2:14-15 - Forasmuch then as the children are partakers of flesh and blood, he also himself likewise took part of the same; that through death he might destroy him that had the power of death, that is, the devil; And deliver them who through fear of death were all their lifetime subject to bondage.

2 PETER 2:9 - The Lord knoweth how to deliver the godly out of temptations, and to reserve the unjust unto the day of judgment to be punished:

2 TIMOTHY 3:10-11 - But thou hast fully known my doctrine, manner of life, purpose, faith, longsuffering, charity, patience, Persecutions, afflictions, which came unto me at Antioch, at Iconium, at Lystra; what persecutions I endured: but out of them all the Lord delivered me.

DISCOURAGEMENT

NEHEMIAH 8:10 - Then he said unto them, Go your way, eat the fat, and drink the sweet, and send portions unto them for whom nothing is prepared: for this day is holy unto our Lord: neither be ye sorry; for the joy of the LORD is your strength.

PSALMS 9:9-10 - The LORD also will be a refuge for the oppressed, a refuge in times of trouble. And they that know thy name will put their trust in thee: for thou, LORD, hast not forsaken them that seek thee.

PSALMS 27:13-14 - I had fainted, unless I had believed to see the goodness of the LORD in the land of the living. Wait on the LORD: be of good courage, and he shall strengthen thine heart: wait, I say, on the LORD.

PSALMS 30:5 - For his anger endureth but a moment; in his favour is life: weeping may endure for a night, but joy cometh in the morning.

PSALMS 31:23-24 - O love the LORD, all ye his saints: for the LORD preserveth the faithful, and plentifully rewardeth the proud doer. Be of good courage, and he shall strengthen your heart, all ye that hope in the LORD.

PSALMS 37:23-25 - The steps of a good man are ordered by the LORD: and he delighteth in his way. Though he fall, he shall not be utterly cast down: for the LORD upholdeth him with his hand. I have been young, and now am old; yet have I not seen the righteous forsaken, nor his seed begging bread.

PSALMS 42:11 - Why art thou cast down, O my soul? and why art thou disquieted within me? hope thou in God: for I shall yet praise him, who is the health of my countenance, and my God.

PSALMS 138:8 - The LORD will perfect that which concerneth me: thy mercy, O LORD, endureth for ever: forsake not the works of thine own hands.

PSALMS 147:3 - He healeth the broken in heart, and bindeth up their wounds.

ISAIAH 40:31 - But they that wait upon the LORD shall renew their strength; they shall mount up with wings as eagles; they shall run, and not be weary; and they shall walk, and not faint.

ISAIAH 50:10 - Who is among you that feareth the LORD, that obeyeth the voice of his servant, that walketh in darkness, and hath no light? let him trust in the name of the LORD, and stay upon his God.

ISAIAH 51:11 - Therefore the redeemed of the LORD shall return, and come with singing unto Zion; and everlasting joy shall be upon their head: they shall obtain gladness and joy; and sorrow and mourning shall flee away.

MATTHEW 11:28-30 - Come unto me, all ye that labour and are heavy laden, and I will give you rest. Take my yoke upon you, and learn of me; for I am meek and lowly in heart: and ye shall find rest unto your souls. For my yoke is easy, and my burden is light.

LUKE 18:1 - And he spake a parable unto them to this end, that men ought always to pray, and not to faint;

ROMANS 8:38-39 - For I am persuaded, that neither death, nor life, nor angels, nor principalities, nor powers, nor things present, nor things to come, Nor height, nor depth, nor any other creature, shall be able to separate us from the love of God, which is in Christ Jesus our Lord.

1 CORNITHIANS 15:58 - Therefore, my beloved brethren, be ye stedfast, unmoveable, always abounding in the work of the Lord, forasmuch as ye know that your labour is not in vain in the Lord.

2 CORNITHIANS 1:3-4 - Blessed be God, even the Father of our Lord Jesus Christ, the Father of mercies, and the God of all comfort; Who comforteth us in all our tribulation, that we may be able to comfort them which are in any trouble, by the comfort wherewith we ourselves are comforted of God.

2 CORINTHIANS 4:8-9 - We are troubled on every side, yet not distressed; we are perplexed, but not in despair; Persecuted, but not forsaken; cast down, but not destroyed;

GALATIANS 6:9 - And let us not be weary in well doing: for in due season we shall reap, if we faint not.

PHILIPPIANS 1:6 - Being confident of this very thing, that he which hath begun a good work in you will perform it until the day of Jesus Christ:

PHILIPPIANS 4:8 - Finally, brethren, whatsoever things are true, whatsoever things are honest, whatsoever things are just, whatsoever things are pure, whatsoever things are lovely, whatsoever things are of good report; if there be any virtue, and if there be any praise, think on these things.

HEBREWS 4:14-16 - Seeing then that we have a great high priest, that is passed into the heavens, Jesus the Son of God, let us hold fast our profession. For we have not an high priest which cannot be touched with the feeling of our infirmities; but was in all points tempted like as we are, yet without sin. Let us therefore come boldly unto the throne of grace, that we may obtain mercy, and find grace to help in time of need.

HEBREWS 6:10 - For God is not unrighteous to forget your work and labour of love, which ye have showed toward his name, in that ye have ministered to the saints, and do minister.

HEBREWS 10:35-36 - Cast not away therefore your confidence, which hath great recompense of reward. For ye have need of patience, that, after ye have done the will of God, ye might receive the promise.

JAMES 4:8 - Draw nigh to God, and he will draw nigh to you. Cleanse your hands, ye sinners; and purify your hearts, ye double minded.

1 PETER 4:12-13 - Beloved, think it not strange concerning the fiery trial which is to try you, as though some strange thing happened unto you: But rejoice, inasmuch as ye are partakers of Christ's sufferings; that, when his glory shall be revealed, ye may be glad also with exceeding joy.

EMERGENCIES
BLEEDING – TO STOP

EZEKIEL 16:6 - And when I passed by thee, and saw thee polluted in thine own blood, I said unto thee when thou wast in thy blood, Live; yea, I said unto thee when thou wast in thy blood, Live.

BROKEN BONES – PROTECTION FROM

PSALMS 34:20 - He keepeth all his bones: not one of them is broken.

BURNS – PROTECTION FROM

ISAIAH 43:2 - When thou passest through the waters, I will be with thee; and through the rivers, they shall not overflow thee: when thou walkest through the fire, thou shalt not be burned; neither shall the flame kindle upon thee.

CRIME- PROTECTION FROM

PSALMS 91:5 - Thou shalt not be afraid for the terror by night; nor for the arrow that flieth by day;

PSALMS 91:10 - There shall no evil befall thee, neither shall any plague come nigh thy dwelling.

EPIDEMICS OR CONTAGIOUS DISEASE – PROTECTION FROM

PSALMS 91:9-10 - Because thou hast made the LORD, which is my refuge, even the most High, thy habitation; There shall no evil befall thee, neither shall any plague come nigh thy dwelling.

EXTERMINATION OF INSECTS, ROACHES, MOSQUITOES

PSALMS 91:5-6 - Thou shalt not be afraid for the terror by night; nor for the arrow that flieth by day; Nor for the pestilence that walketh in darkness; nor for the destruction that wasteth at noonday.

FIRE – PROTECTION FROM

ISAIAH 43:2 - When thou passest through the waters, I will be with thee; and through the rivers, they shall not overflow thee: when thou walkest through the fire, thou shalt not be burned; neither shall the flame kindle upon thee.

FLOOD – PROTECTION FROM

ISAIAH 43:2 - When thou passest through the waters, I will be with thee; and through the rivers, they shall not overflow thee: when thou walkest through the fire, thou shalt not be burned; neither shall the flame kindle upon thee.

PAIN – FREEDOM FROM

LUKE 10:19 - Behold, I give unto you power to tread on serpents and scorpions, and over all the power of the enemy: and nothing shall by any means hurt you.

SNAKE BITES (ALL INSECT BITES) AND POISON – FREEDOM FROM

MARK 16:17-18 - And these signs shall follow them that believe; In my name shall they cast out devils; they shall speak with new tongues; They shall take up serpents; and if they drink any deadly thing, it shall not hurt them; they shall lay hands on the sick, and they shall recover.

STORMS AND TORNADOES – PROTECTION FROM

ISAIAH 32:2 - And a man shall be as an hiding place from the wind, and a covert from the tempest; as rivers of water in a dry place, as the shadow of a great rock in a weary land.

MARK 4:39 - And he arose, and rebuked the wind, and said unto the sea, Peace, be still. And the wind ceased, and there was a great calm.

JOHN 14:12 - Verily, verily, I say unto you, He that believeth on me, the works that I do shall he do also; and greater works than these shall he do; because I go unto my Father.

WARTIME – PROTECTION FROM

PSALMS 91:7-8 - A thousand shall fall at thy side, and ten thousand at thy right hand; but it shall not come nigh thee. Only with thine eyes shalt thou behold and see the reward of the wicked.

DEUTERONOMY 28:7 - The LORD shall cause thine enemies that rise up against thee to be smitten before thy face: they shall come out against thee one way, and flee before thee seven ways.

FAITH

MATTHEW 9:29 - Then touched he their eyes, saying, According to your faith be it unto you.

MATTHEW 17:20 - And Jesus said unto them, Because of your unbelief: for verily I say unto you, If ye have faith as a grain of mustard seed, ye shall say unto this mountain, Remove hence to yonder place; and it shall remove; and nothing shall be impossible unto you.

MARK 9:23 - Jesus said unto him, If thou canst believe, all things are possible to him that believeth.

MARK 11:22-23 - And Jesus answering saith unto them, Have faith in God. For verily I say unto you, That whosoever shall say unto this mountain, Be thou removed, and be thou cast into the sea; and shall not doubt in his heart, but shall believe that those things which he saith shall come to pass; he shall have whatsoever he saith.

ROMANS 4:5 - But to him that worketh not, but believeth on him that justifieth the ungodly, his faith is counted for righteousness.

ROMANS 5:1 - Therefore being justified by faith, we have peace with God through our Lord Jesus Christ:

ROMANS 10:17 - So then faith cometh by hearing, and hearing by the word of God.

ROMANS 12:3 - For I say, through the grace given unto me, to every man that is among you, not to think of himself more highly than he ought to think; but to think soberly, according as God hath dealt to every man the measure of faith.

ROMANS 14:23 - And he that doubteth is damned if he eat, because he eateth not of faith: for whatsoever is not of faith is sin.

2 CORINTHIANS 1:24 - Not for that we have dominion over your faith, but are helpers of your joy: for by faith ye stand.

2 CORINTHIANS 4:13 - We having the same spirit of faith, according as it is written, I believed, and therefore have I spoken; we also believe, and therefore speak;

GALATIANS 5:6 - For in Jesus Christ neither circumcision availeth any thing, nor uncircumcision; but faith which worketh by love.

EPHESIANS 2:8-9 - For by grace are ye saved through faith; and that not of yourselves: it is the gift of God: Not of works, lest any man should boast.

2 THESSALONIANS 1:3 - We are bound to thank God always for you, brethren, as it is meet, because that your faith groweth exceedingly, and the charity of every one of you all toward each other aboundeth;

PHILEMON 1:6 - That the communication of thy faith may become effectual by the acknowledging of every good thing which is in you in Christ Jesus.

HEBREWS 6:11-12 - And we desire that every one of you do show the same diligence to the full assurance of hope unto the end: That ye be not slothful, but followers of them who through faith and patience inherit the promises.

HEBREWS 10:38 - Now the just shall live by faith: but if any man draw back, my soul shall have no pleasure in him.

HEBREWS 11:1 - Now faith is the substance of things hoped for, the evidence of things not seen.

HEBREWS 11:6 - But without faith it is impossible to please him: for he that cometh to God must believe that he is, and that he is a rewarder of them that diligently seek him.

JAMES 1:2-3 - My brethren, count it all joy when ye fall into divers temptations; Knowing this, that the trying of your faith worketh patience.

JUDE 1:20 - But ye, beloved, building up yourselves on your most holy faith, praying in the Holy Ghost,

FAVOR

PSALMS 5:12 - For thou, LORD, wilt bless the righteous; with favour wilt thou compass him as with a shield.

PSALMS 41:11 - By this I know that thou favourest me, because mine enemy doth not triumph over me.

PSALMS 106:44 - Nevertheless he regarded their affliction, when he heard their cry:

PSALMS 119:58 - I entreated thy favour with my whole heart: be merciful unto me according to thy word.

PROVERBS 3:3-4 - Let not mercy and truth forsake thee: bind them about thy neck; write them upon the table of thine heart: So shalt thou find favour and good understanding in the sight of God and man.

PROVERBS 8:33,35 - Hear instruction, and be wise, and refuse it not. For whoso findeth me findeth life, and shall obtain favour of the LORD.

PROVERBS 11:27 - He that diligently seeketh good procureth favour: but he that seeketh mischief, it shall come unto him.

PROVERBS 12:2 - A good man obtaineth favour of the LORD: but a man of wicked devices will he condemn.

PROVERBS 12:22 - Lying lips are abomination to the LORD: but they that deal truly are his delight.

PROVERBS 13:15 - Good understanding giveth favour: but the way of transgressors is hard.

PROVERBS 14:9 - Fools make a mock at sin: but among the righteous there is favour.

PROVERBS 18:22 - Whoso findeth a wife findeth a good thing, and obtaineth favour of the LORD.

PROVERBS 22:1 - A good name is rather to be chosen than great riches, and loving favour rather than silver and gold.

PROVERBS 28:23 - He that rebuketh a man afterwards shall find more favour than he that flattereth with the tongue.

ECCLESIASTES 5:8 - If thou seest the oppression of the poor, and violent perverting of judgment and justice in a province, marvel not at the matter: for he that is higher than the highest regardeth; and there be higher than they.

FEAR

EXODUS 14:13 - And Moses said unto the people, Fear ye not, stand still, and see the salvation of the LORD, which he will show to you to day: for the Egyptians whom ye have seen to day, ye shall see them again no more for ever.

LEVITICUS 26:3-6 - If ye walk in my statutes, and keep my commandments, and do them; Then I will give you rain in due season, and the land shall yield her increase, and the trees of the field shall yield their fruit. And your threshing shall reach unto the vintage, and the vintage shall reach unto the sowing time: and ye shall eat your bread to the full, and dwell in your land safely. And I will give peace in the land, and ye shall lie down, and none shall make you afraid: and I will rid evil beasts out of the land, neither shall the sword go through your land.

DEUTERONOMY 31:6 - Be strong and of a good courage, fear not, nor be afraid of them: for the LORD thy God, he it is that doth go with thee; he will not fail thee, nor forsake thee.

JOSHUA 1:9 - Have not I commanded thee? Be strong and of a good courage; be not afraid, neither be thou dismayed: for the LORD thy God is with thee whithersoever thou goest.

2 KINGS 6:16 - And he answered, Fear not: for they that be with us are more than they that be with them.

PSALMS 23:4 - Yea, though I walk through the valley of the shadow of death, I will fear no evil: for thou art with me; thy rod and thy staff they comfort me.

PSALMS 27:1 - The LORD is my light and my salvation; whom shall I fear? the LORD is the strength of my life; of whom shall I be afraid?

PSALMS 34:4 - I sought the LORD, and he heard me, and delivered me from all my fears.

PSALMS 46:1-2 - God is our refuge and strength, a very present help in trouble. Therefore will not we fear, though the earth be removed, and though the mountains be carried into the midst of the sea;

PSALMS 56:4 - In God I will praise his word, in God I have put my trust; I will not fear what flesh can do unto me.

PSALMS 64:1 - Hear my voice, O God, in my prayer: preserve my life from fear of the enemy.

PSALMS 91:5-6 -Thou shalt not be afraid for the terror by night; nor for the arrow that flieth by day; Nor for the pestilence that walketh in darkness; nor for the destruction that wasteth at noonday.

PSALMS 112:6-7 - Surely he shall not be moved for ever: the righteous shall be in everlasting remembrance. He shall not be afraid of evil tidings: his heart is fixed, trusting in the LORD.

PSALMS 118:6 - The LORD is on my side; I will not fear: what can man do unto me?

PROVERBS 1:33 - But whoso hearkeneth unto me shall dwell safely, and shall be quiet from fear of evil.

PROVERBS 3:25-26 - Be not afraid of sudden fear, neither of the desolation of the wicked, when it cometh. For the LORD shall be thy confidence, and shall keep thy foot from being taken.

PROVERBS 29:25 - The fear of man bringeth a snare: but whoso putteth his trust in the LORD shall be safe.

ISAIAH 12:2 - Behold, God is my salvation; I will trust, and not be afraid: for the LORD JEHOVAH is my strength and my song; he also is become my salvation.

ISAIAH 35:4 - Say to them that are of a fearful heart, Be strong, fear not: behold, your God will come with vengeance, even God with a recompense; he will come and save you.

ISAIAH 41:10 - Fear thou not; for I am with thee: be not dismayed; for I am thy God: I will strengthen thee; yea, I will help thee; yea, I will uphold thee with the right hand of my righteousness.

ROMANS 8:15 - For ye have not received the spirit of bondage again to fear; but ye have received the Spirit of adoption, whereby we cry, Abba, Father.

PHILIPPIANS 1:27-28 - Only let your conversation be as it becometh the gospel of Christ: that whether I come and see you, or else be absent, I may hear of your affairs, that ye stand fast in one spirit, with one mind striving together for the faith of the gospel; And in nothing terrified by your adversaries: which is to them an evident token of perdition, but to you of salvation, and that of God.

2 TIMOTHY 1:7 - For God hath not given us the spirit of fear; but of power, and of love, and of a sound mind.

HEBREWS 13:5-6 - Let your conversation be without covetousness; and be content with such things as ye have: for he hath said, I will never leave thee, nor forsake thee. So that we may boldly say, The Lord is my helper, and I will not fear what man shall do unto me.

1 JOHN 2:5 - But whoso keepeth his word, in him verily is the love of God perfected: hereby know we that we are in him.

1 JOHN 4:18 - There is no fear in love; but perfect love casteth out fear: because fear hath torment. He that feareth is not made perfect in love.

FORGIVENESS

2 CHRONICLES 6:21 - Hearken therefore unto the supplications of thy servant, and of thy people Israel, which they shall make toward this place: hear thou from thy dwelling place, even from heaven; and when thou hearest, forgive.

NEHEMIAH 9:17 - And refused to obey, neither were mindful of thy wonders that thou didst among them; but hardened their necks, and in their rebellion appointed a captain to return to their bondage: but thou art a God ready to pardon, gracious and merciful, slow to anger, and of great kindness, and forsookest them not.

PSALMS 25:11 - For thy name's sake, O LORD, pardon mine iniquity; for it is great.

PSALMS 32:1-2 - Blessed is he whose transgression is forgiven, whose sin is covered. Blessed is the man unto whom the LORD imputeth not iniquity, and in whose spirit there is no guile.

PSALMS 85:2 - Thou hast forgiven the iniquity of thy people, thou hast covered all their sin. Selah.

PSALMS 86:5 - For thou, Lord, art good, and ready to forgive; and plenteous in mercy unto all them that call upon thee.

PSALMS 103:2-3 - Bless the LORD, O my soul, and forget not all his benefits: Who forgiveth all thine iniquities; who healeth all thy diseases;

PSALMS 103:10-12 - He hath not dealt with us after our sins; nor rewarded us according to our iniquities. For as the heaven is high above the earth, so great is his mercy toward them that fear him. As far as the east is from the west, so far hath he removed our transgressions from us.

PSALMS 130:3-4 - If thou, LORD, shouldest mark iniquities, O Lord, who shall stand? But there is forgiveness with thee, that thou mayest be feared.

ISAIAH 55:6-7 - Seek ye the LORD while he may be found, call ye upon him while he is near: Let the wicked forsake his way, and the unrighteous man his thoughts: and let him return unto the LORD, and he will have mercy upon him; and to our God, for he will abundantly pardon.

JEREMIAH 31:33-34 - But this shall be the covenant that I will make with the house of Israel; After those days, saith the LORD, I will put my law in their inward parts, and write it in their hearts; and will be their God, and they shall be my people. And they shall teach no more every man his neighbour, and every man his brother, saying, Know the LORD: for they shall all know me, from the least of them unto the greatest of them, saith the LORD: for I will forgive their iniquity, and I will remember their sin no more.

MICAH 7:18-19 - Who is a God like unto thee, that pardoneth iniquity, and passeth by the transgression of the remnant of his heritage? he retaineth not his anger for ever, because he delighteth in mercy. He will turn again, he will have compassion upon us; he will subdue our iniquities; and thou wilt cast all their sins into the depths of the sea.

MATTHEW 6:12 - And forgive us our debts, as we forgive our debtors.

MATTHEW 18:21-22 - Then came Peter to him, and said, Lord, how oft shall my brother sin against me, and I forgive him? till seven times? Jesus saith unto him, I say not unto thee, Until seven times: but, Until seventy times seven.

MARK 11:25-26 - And when ye stand praying, forgive, if ye have ought against any: that your Father also which is in heaven may forgive you your trespasses. But if ye do not forgive, neither will your Father which is in heaven forgive your trespasses.

LUKE 6:37 - Judge not, and ye shall not be judged: condemn not, and ye shall not be condemned: forgive, and ye shall be forgiven:

LUKE 24:46-47 - And said unto them, Thus it is written, and thus it behoved Christ to suffer, and to rise from the dead the third day: And that repentance and remission of sins should be preached in his name among all nations, beginning at Jerusalem.

JOHN 20:23 - Whose soever sins ye remit, they are remitted unto them; and whose soever sins ye retain, they are retained.

ACTS 10:38,43 - How God anointed Jesus of Nazareth with the Holy Ghost and with power: who went about doing good, and healing all that were oppressed of the devil; for God was with him. To him give all the prophets witness, that through his name whosoever believeth in him shall receive remission of sins.

EPHESIANS 1:3,7 - Blessed be the God and Father of our Lord Jesus Christ, who hath blessed us with all spiritual blessings in heavenly places in Christ: In whom we have redemption through his blood, the forgiveness of sins, according to the riches of his grace;

EPHESIANS 4:32 - And be ye kind one to another, tenderhearted, forgiving one another, even as God for Christ's sake hath forgiven you.

COLOSSIANS 2:13 - And you, being dead in your sins and the uncircumcision of your flesh, hath he quickened together with him, having forgiven you all trespasses;

HEBREWS 9:22 - And almost all things are by the law purged with blood; and without shedding of blood is no remission.

JAMES 5:15 - And the prayer of faith shall save the sick, and the Lord shall raise him up; and if he have committed sins, they shall be forgiven him.

1 JOHN 1:9 - If we confess our sins, he is faithful and just to forgive us our sins, and to cleanse us from all unrighteousness.

1 JOHN 2:1-2 - My little children, these things write I unto you, that ye sin not. And if any man sin, we have an advocate with the Father, Jesus Christ the righteous: And he is the propitiation for our sins: and not for ours only, but also for the sins of the whole world.

SCRIPTURES TO LIVE BY

GUIDANCE

DEUTERONOMY 31:8 - And the LORD, he it is that doth go before thee; he will be with thee, he will not fail thee, neither forsake thee: fear not, neither be dismayed.

PSALMS 16:7 - I will bless the LORD, who hath given me counsel: my reins also instruct me in the night seasons.

PSALMS 16:11 - Thou wilt show me the path of life: in thy presence is fulness of joy; at thy right hand there are pleasures for evermore.

PSALMS 17:5 - Hold up my goings in thy paths, that my footsteps slip not.

PSALMS 18:28 - For thou wilt light my candle: the LORD my God will enlighten my darkness.

PSALMS 23:1-3 - The LORD is my shepherd; I shall not want. He maketh me to lie down in green pastures: he leadeth me beside the still waters. He restoreth my soul: he leadeth me in the paths of righteousness for his name's sake.

PSALMS 25:9 - The meek will he guide in judgment: and the meek will he teach his way.

PSALMS 31:3 - For thou art my rock and my fortress; therefore for thy name's sake lead me, and guide me.

PSALMS 32:8 - I will instruct thee and teach thee in the way which thou shalt go: I will guide thee with mine eye.

PSALMS 37:5 - Commit thy way unto the LORD; trust also in him; and he shall bring it to pass.

PSALMS 37:23-24 - The steps of a good man are ordered by the LORD: and he delighteth in his way. Though he fall, he shall not be utterly cast down: for the LORD upholdeth him with his hand.

PSALMS 43:3 - O send out thy light and thy truth: let them lead me; let them bring me unto thy holy hill, and to thy tabernacles.

PSALMS 48:14 - For this God is our God for ever and ever: he will be our guide even unto death.

PSALMS 73:24 - Thou shalt guide me with thy counsel, and afterward receive me to glory.

PSALMS 85:13 - Righteousness shall go before him; and shall set us in the way of his steps.

PSALMS 107:7 - And he led them forth by the right way, that they might go to a city of habitation.

PSALMS 112:5 - A good man showeth favour, and lendeth: he will guide his affairs with discretion.

PSALMS 119:105 - Thy word is a lamp unto my feet, and a light unto my path.

PSALMS 139:9-10 - If I take the wings of the morning, and dwell in the uttermost parts of the sea; Even there shall thy hand lead me, and thy right hand shall hold me.

PSALMS 139:23-24 - Search me, O God, and know my heart: try me, and know my thoughts: And see if there be any wicked way in me, and lead me in the way everlasting.

PSALMS 143:8 - Cause me to hear thy lovingkindness in the morning; for in thee do I trust: cause me to know the way wherein I should walk; for I lift up my soul unto thee.

PSALMS 143:10 - Teach me to do thy will; for thou art my God: thy spirit is good; lead me into the land of uprightness.

PROVERBS 3:5-6 - Trust in the LORD with all thine heart; and lean not unto thine own understanding. In all thy ways acknowledge him, and he shall direct thy paths.

PROVERBS 4:18 - But the path of the just is as the shining light, that shineth more and more unto the perfect day.

PROVERBS 4:26-27 - Ponder the path of thy feet, and let all thy ways be established. Turn not to the right hand nor to the left: remove thy foot from evil.

PROVERBS 6:20-22 - My son, keep thy father's commandment, and forsake not the law of thy mother: Bind them continually upon thine heart, and tie them about thy neck. When thou goest, it shall lead thee; when thou sleepest, it shall keep thee; and when thou awakest, it shall talk with thee.

PROVERBS 8:20-21 - I lead in the way of righteousness, in the midst of the paths of judgment: That I may cause those that love me to inherit substance; and I will fill their treasures.

PROVERBS 11:3 - The integrity of the upright shall guide them: but the perverseness of transgressors shall destroy them.

PROVERBS 11:5 - The righteousness of the perfect shall direct his way: but the wicked shall fall by his own wickedness.

PROVERBS 15:19 - The way of the slothful man is as an hedge of thorns: but the way of the righteous is made plain.

PROVERBS 16:9 - A man's heart deviseth his way: but the LORD directeth his steps.

PROVERBS 20:27 - The spirit of man is the candle of the LORD, searching all the inward parts of the belly.

ECCLESIASTES 10:10 - If the iron be blunt, and he do not whet the edge, then must he put to more strength: but wisdom is profitable to direct.

JEREMIAH 31:9 - They shall come with weeping, and with supplications will I lead them: I will cause them to walk by the rivers of waters in a straight way, wherein they shall not stumble: for I am a father to Israel, and Ephraim is my firstborn.

ISAIAH 30:21 – And thine ears shall hear a word behind thee, saying, This is the way, walk ye in it, when ye turn to the right hand, and when ye turn to the left.

ISAIAH 45:12-13 - I have made the earth, and created man upon it: I, even my hands, have stretched out the heavens, and all their host have I commanded. I have raised him up in righteousness, and I will direct all his ways: he shall build my city, and he shall let go my captives, not for price nor reward, saith the LORD of hosts.

ISAIAH 55:12 - For ye shall go out with joy, and be led forth with peace: the mountains and the hills shall break forth before you into singing, and all the trees of the field shall clap their hands.

ISAIAH 58:11 - And the LORD shall guide thee continually, and satisfy thy soul in drought, and make fat thy bones: and thou shalt be like a watered garden, and like a spring of water, whose waters fail not.

ISAIAH 61:8 - For I the LORD love judgment, I hate robbery for burnt offering; and I will direct their work in truth, and I will make an everlasting covenant with them.

MATTHEW 6:13 - And lead us not into temptation, but deliver us from evil: For thine is the kingdom, and the power, and the glory, for ever. Amen.

JOHN 10:27 - My sheep hear my voice, and I know them, and they follow me:

JOHN 16:13 - Howbeit when he, the Spirit of truth, is come, he will guide you into all truth: for he shall not speak of himself; but whatsoever he shall hear, that shall he speak: and he will show you things to come.

ROMANS 2:4 - Or despisest thou the riches of his goodness and forbearance and longsuffering; not knowing that the goodness of God leadeth thee to repentance?

ROMANS 8:14 - For as many as are led by the Spirit of God, they are the sons of God.

GALATIANS 5:18 - But if ye be led of the Spirit, ye are not under the law.

COLOSSIANS 3:15 - And let the peace of God rule in your hearts, to the which also ye are called in one body; and be ye thankful.

2 THESSALONIANS 3:5 - And the Lord direct your hearts into the love of God, and into the patient waiting for Christ.

HEALING

EXODUS 15:26 - And said, If thou wilt diligently hearken to the voice of the LORD thy God, and wilt do that which is right in his sight, and wilt give ear to his commandments, and keep all his statutes, I will put none of these diseases upon thee, which I have brought upon the Egyptians: for I am the LORD that healeth thee.

EXODUS 23:25-26 - And ye shall serve the LORD your God, and he shall bless thy bread, and thy water; and I will take sickness away from the midst of thee. There shall nothing cast their young, nor be barren, in thy land: the number of thy days I will fulfil.

PSALMS 30:2 - O LORD my God, I cried unto thee, and thou hast healed me.

PSALMS 42:11 - Why art thou cast down, O my soul? and why art thou disquieted within me? hope thou in God: for I shall yet praise him, who is the health of my countenance, and my God.

PSALMS 67:1-2 - God be merciful unto us, and bless us; and cause his face to shine upon us; Selah. That thy way may be known upon earth, thy saving health among all nations.

PSALMS 91:10 - There shall no evil befall thee, neither shall any plague come nigh thy dwelling.

PSALMS 103:2-3 - Bless the LORD, O my soul, and forget not all his benefits: Who forgiveth all thine iniquities; who healeth all thy diseases;

PSALMS 105:37 - He brought them forth also with silver and gold: and there was not one feeble person among their tribes.

PSALMS 107:20 - He sent his word, and healed them, and delivered them from their destructions.

PSALMS 128:1-2 - Blessed is every one that feareth the LORD; that walketh in his ways. For thou shalt eat the labour of thine hands: happy shalt thou be, and it shall be well with thee.

PSALMS 147:3 - He healeth the broken in heart, and bindeth up their wounds.

PROVERBS 3:7-8 - Be not wise in thine own eyes: fear the LORD, and depart from evil. It shall be health to thy navel, and marrow to thy bones.

PROVERBS 4:20-22 - My son, attend to my words; incline thine ear unto my sayings. Let them not depart from thine eyes; keep them in the midst of thine heart. For they are life unto those that find them, and health to all their flesh.

PROVERBS 12:18 - There is that speaketh like the piercings of a sword: but the tongue of the wise is health.

PROVERBS 13:17 - A wicked messenger falleth into mischief: but a faithful ambassador is health.

PROVERBS 14:30 - A sound heart is the life of the flesh: but envy the rottenness of the bones.

PROVERBS 16:24 - Pleasant words are as an honeycomb, sweet to the soul, and health to the bones.

PROVERBS 17:22 - A merry heart doeth good like a medicine: but a broken spirit drieth the bones.

ISAIAH 53:5 - But he was wounded for our transgressions, he was bruised for our iniquities: the chastisement of our peace was upon him; and with his stripes we are healed.

ISAIAH 57:19 - I create the fruit of the lips; Peace, peace to him that is far off, and to him that is near, saith the LORD; and I will heal him.

ISAIAH 58:8 - Then shall thy light break forth as the morning, and thine health shall spring forth speedily: and thy righteousness shall go before thee; the glory of the LORD shall be thy rereward.

JEREMIAH 17:14 - Heal me, O LORD, and I shall be healed; save me, and I shall be saved: for thou art my praise.

JEREMIAH 30:17 - For I will restore health unto thee, and I will heal thee of thy wounds, saith the LORD; because they called thee an Outcast, saying, This is Zion, whom no man seeketh after.

MALACHI 4:2 - But unto you that fear my name shall the Sun of righteousness arise with healing in his wings; and ye shall go forth, and grow up as calves of the stall.

MATTHEW 8:16-17 - When the even was come, they brought unto him many that were possessed with devils: and he cast out the spirits with his word, and healed all that were sick: That it might be fulfilled which was spoken by Esaias the prophet, saying, Himself took our infirmities, and bare our sicknesses.

MARK 11:24 - Therefore I say unto you, What things soever ye desire, when ye pray, believe that ye receive them, and ye shall have them.

MARK 16:17-18 - And these signs shall follow them that believe; In my name shall they cast out devils; they shall speak with new tongues; They shall take up serpents; and if they drink any deadly thing, it shall not hurt them; they shall lay hands on the sick, and they shall recover.

LUKE 4:18 - The Spirit of the Lord is upon me, because he hath anointed me to preach the gospel to the poor; he hath sent me to heal the brokenhearted, to preach deliverance to the captives, and recovering of sight to the blind, to set at liberty them that are bruised,

JOHN 10:10 - The thief cometh not, but for to steal, and to kill, and to destroy: I am come that they might have life, and that they might have it more abundantly.

ACTS 10:38 - How God anointed Jesus of Nazareth with the Holy Ghost and with power: who went about doing good, and healing all that were oppressed of the devil; for God was with him.

ROMANS 8:2 - For the law of the Spirit of life in Christ Jesus hath made me free from the law of sin and death.

ROMANS 8:11 - But if the Spirit of him that raised up Jesus from the dead dwell in you, he that raised up Christ from the dead shall also quicken your mortal bodies by his Spirit that dwelleth in you.

ROMANS 8:26-27 - Likewise the Spirit also helpeth our infirmities: for we know not what we should pray for as we ought: but the Spirit itself maketh intercession for us with groanings which cannot be uttered. And he that searcheth the hearts knoweth what is the mind of the Spirit, because he maketh intercession for the saints according to the will of God.

ROMANS 8:34 - Who is he that condemneth? It is Christ that died, yea rather, that is risen again, who is even at the right hand of God, who also maketh intercession for us.

GALATIANS 3:13-14 - Christ hath redeemed us from the curse of the law, being made a curse for us: for it is written, Cursed is every one that hangeth on a tree: That the blessing of Abraham might come on the Gentiles through Jesus Christ; that we might receive the promise of the Spirit through faith.

EPHESIANS 6:1,3 - Children, obey your parents in the Lord: for this is right. That it may be well with thee, and thou mayest live long on the earth.

JAMES 5:14-16 - Is any sick among you? let him call for the elders of the church; and let them pray over him, anointing him with oil in the name of the Lord: And the prayer of faith shall save the sick, and the Lord shall raise him up; and if he have committed sins, they shall be forgiven him. Confess your faults one to another, and pray one for another, that ye may be healed. The effectual fervent prayer of a righteous man availeth much.

1 PETER 2:24 - Who his own self bare our sins in his own body on the tree, that we, being dead to sins, should live unto righteousness: by whose stripes ye were healed.

3 JOHN 1:2 - Beloved, I wish above all things that thou mayest prosper and be in health, even as thy soul prospereth.

THE HOLY SPIRIT
(GIFT OF)

ISAIAH 28:11 - For with stammering lips and another tongue will he speak to this people.

JOEL 2:28-29 - And it shall come to pass afterward, that I will pour out my spirit upon all flesh; and your sons and your daughters shall prophesy, your old men shall dream dreams, your young men shall see visions: And also upon the servants and upon the handmaids in those days will I pour out my spirit.

MARK 16:17 - And these signs shall follow them that believe; In my name shall they cast out devils; they shall speak with new tongues;

LUKE 3:16 - John answered, saying unto them all, I indeed baptize you with water; but one mightier than I cometh, the latchet of whose shoes I am not worthy to unloose: he shall baptize you with the Holy Ghost and with fire:

LUKE 11:13 - If ye then, being evil, know how to give good gifts unto your children: how much more shall your heavenly Father give the Holy Spirit to them that ask him?

LUKE 24:49 - And, behold, I send the promise of my Father upon you: but tarry ye in the city of Jerusalem, until ye be endued with power from on high.

JOHN 14:16-17 - And I will pray the Father, and he shall give you another Comforter, that he may abide with you for ever; Even the Spirit of truth; whom the world cannot receive, because it seeth him not, neither knoweth him: but ye know him; for he dwelleth with you, and shall be in you.

JOHN 7:38-39 - He that believeth on me, as the scripture hath said, out of his belly shall flow rivers of living water. (But this spake he of the Spirit, which they that believe on him should receive: for the Holy Ghost was not yet given; because that Jesus was not yet glorified.)

ACTS 1:8 - But ye shall receive power, after that the Holy Ghost is come upon you: and ye shall be witnesses unto me both in Jerusalem, and in all Judaea, and in Samaria, and unto the uttermost part of the earth.

ACTS 2:1,4 - And when the day of Pentecost was fully come, they were all with one accord in one place. And they were all filled with the Holy Ghost, and began to speak with other tongues, as the Spirit gave them utterance.

ACTS 2:38-39 - Then Peter said unto them, Repent, and be baptized every one of you in the name of Jesus Christ for the remission of sins, and ye shall receive the gift of the Holy Ghost. For the promise is unto you, and to your children, and to all that are afar off, even as many as the Lord our God shall call.

ACTS 8:14,15,17 - Now when the apostles which were at Jerusalem heard that Samaria had received the word of God, they sent unto them Peter and John: Who, when they were come down, prayed for them, that they might receive the Holy Ghost: Then laid they their hands on them, and they received the Holy Ghost.

ACTS 10:44-46 - While Peter yet spake these words, the Holy Ghost fell on all them which heard the word. And they of the circumcision which believed were astonished, as many as came with Peter, because that on the Gentiles also was poured out the gift of the Holy Ghost. For they heard them speak with tongues, and magnify God. Then answered Peter,

ACTS 19:2,6 - He said unto them, Have ye received the Holy Ghost since ye believed? And they said unto him, We have not so much as heard whether there be any Holy Ghost. And when Paul had laid his hands upon them, the Holy Ghost came on them; and they spake with tongues, and prophesied.

1 CORINTHIANS 14:2 - For he that speaketh in an unknown tongue speaketh not unto men, but unto God: for no man understandeth him; howbeit in the spirit he speaketh mysteries.

1 CORINTHIANS 14:4 - He that speaketh in an unknown tongue edifieth himself; but he that prophesieth edifieth the church.

1 CORINTHIANS 14:5 - I would that ye all spake with tongues, but rather that ye prophesied: for greater is he that prophesieth than he that speaketh with tongues, except he interpret, that the church may receive edifying.

1 CORINTHIANS 14:14 - For if I pray in an un-known tongue, my spirit prayeth, but my understanding is unfruitful.

1 CORINTHIANS 14:39 - Wherefore, brethren, cov-et to prophesy, and forbid not to speak with tongues.

GALATIANS 3:13-14 - Christ hath redeemed us from the curse of the law, being made a curse for us: for it is written, Cursed is every one that hangeth on a tree: That the blessing of Abraham might come on the Gentiles through Jesus Christ; that we might receive the promise of the Spirit through faith.

EPHESIANS 5:18 - And be not drunk with wine, wherein is excess; but be filled with the Spirit;

EPHESIANS 6:18 - Praying always with all prayer and supplication in the Spirit, and watching thereunto with all perseverance and supplication for all saints;

JUDE 1:20 - But ye, beloved, building up yourselves on your most holy faith, praying in the Holy Ghost,

THE HOLY SPIRIT
(MINISTRY OF)

GENESIS 1:1-3 - In the beginning God created the heaven and the earth. And the earth was without form, and void; and darkness was upon the face of the deep. And the Spirit of God moved upon the face of the waters. And God said, Let there be light: and there was light.

ISAIAH 11:2-3 - And the spirit of the LORD shall rest upon him, the spirit of wisdom and understanding, the spirit of counsel and might, the spirit of knowledge and of the fear of the LORD; And shall make him of quick understanding in the fear of the LORD: and he shall not judge after the sight of his eyes, neither reprove after the hearing of his ears:

ISAIAH 59:19 - So shall they fear the name of the LORD from the west, and his glory from the rising of the sun. When the enemy shall come in like a flood, the Spirit of the LORD shall lift up a standard against him.

ZECHARIAH 4:6 - Then he answered and spake unto me, saying, This is the word of the LORD unto Zerubbabel, saying, Not by might, nor by power, but by my spirit, saith the LORD of hosts.

MATTHEW 12:28 - But if I cast out devils by the Spirit of God, then the kingdom of God is come unto you.

JOHN 3:5-6 - Jesus answered, Verily, verily, I say unto thee, Except a man be born of water and of the Spirit, he cannot enter into the kingdom of God. That which is born of the flesh is flesh; and that which is born of the Spirit is spirit.

JOHN 14:26 - But the Comforter, which is the Holy Ghost, whom the Father will send in my name, he shall teach you all things, and bring all things to your remembrance, whatsoever I have said unto you.

JOHN 15:26 - But when the Comforter is come, whom I will send unto you from the Father, even the Spirit of truth, which proceedeth from the Father, he shall testify of me:

JOHN 16:7-8 - Nevertheless I tell you the truth; It is expedient for you that I go away: for if I go not away, the Comforter will not come unto you; but if I depart, I will send him unto you. And when he is come, he will reprove the world of sin, and of righteousness, and of judgment:

JOHN 16:13-14 - Howbeit when he, the Spirit of truth, is come, he will guide you into all truth: for he shall not speak of himself; but whatsoever he shall hear, that shall he speak: and he will show you things to come. He shall glorify me: for he shall receive of mine, and shall show it unto you.

ROMANS 5:5 - And hope maketh not ashamed; because the love of God is shed abroad in our hearts by the Holy Ghost which is given unto us.

ROMANS 8:11 - But if the Spirit of him that raised up Jesus from the dead dwell in you, he that raised up Christ from the dead shall also quicken your mortal bodies by his Spirit that dwelleth in you.

ROMANS 8:16 - The Spirit itself beareth witness with our spirit, that we are the children of God:

ROMANS 8:26-27 - Likewise the Spirit also helpeth our infirmities: for we know not what we should pray for as we ought: but the Spirit itself maketh intercession for us with groanings which cannot be uttered. And he that searcheth the hearts knoweth what is the mind of the Spirit, because he maketh intercession for the saints according to the will of God.

ROMANS 14:17 - For the kingdom of God is not meat and drink; but righteousness, and peace, and joy in the Holy Ghost.

ROMANS 15:16 - That I should be the minister of Jesus Christ to the Gentiles, ministering the gospel of God, that the offering up of the Gentiles might be acceptable, being sanctified by the Holy Ghost.

1 CORINTHIANS 2:4 - And my speech and my preaching was not with enticing words of man's wisdom, but in demonstration of the Spirit and of power:

1 CORINTHIANS 2:9-10,12 - But as it is written, Eye hath not seen, nor ear heard, neither have entered into the heart of man, the things which God hath prepared for them that love him. But God hath revealed them unto us by his Spirit: for the Spirit searcheth all things, yea, the deep things of God. Now we have received, not the spirit of the world, but the spirit which is of God; that we might know the things that are freely given to us of God.

1 CORINTHIANS 3:16 - Know ye not that ye are the temple of God, and that the Spirit of God dwelleth in you?

1 CORINTHIANS 6:19 - What? know ye not that your body is the temple of the Holy Ghost which is in you, which ye have of God, and ye are not your own?

1 CORINTHIANS 12:7 - But the manifestation of the Spirit is given to every man to profit withal.

1 CORINTHIANS 12:11 - But all these worketh that one and the selfsame Spirit, dividing to every man severally as he will.

1 CORINTHIANS 12:13 - For by one Spirit are we all baptized into one body, whether we be Jews or Gentiles, whether we be bond or free; and have been all made to drink into one Spirit.

2 CORINTHIANS 1:21-22 - Now he which stablisheth us with you in Christ, and hath anointed us, is God; Who hath also sealed us, and given the earnest of the Spirit in our hearts.

2 CORINTHIANS 3:17 - Now the Lord is that Spirit: and where the Spirit of the Lord is, there is liberty.

GALATIANS 5:16 - This I say then, Walk in the Spirit, and ye shall not fulfil the lust of the flesh.

GALATIANS 5:18 - But if ye be led of the Spirit, ye are not under the law.

EPHESIANS 1:13-14 - In whom ye also trusted, after that ye heard the word of truth, the gospel of your salvation: in whom also after that ye believed, ye were sealed with that holy Spirit of promise, Which is the earnest of our inheritance until the redemption of the purchased possession, unto the praise of his glory.

EPHESIANS 2:18 - For through him we both have access by one Spirit unto the Father.

EPHESIANS 2:22 - In whom ye also are builded together for an habitation of God through the Spirit.

EPHESIANS 3:16 - That he would grant you, according to the riches of his glory, to be strengthened with might by his Spirit in the inner man;

1 THESSALONIANS 1:5-6 - For our gospel came not unto you in word only, but also in power, and in the Holy Ghost, and in much assurance; as ye know what manner of men we were among you for your sake. And ye became followers of us, and of the Lord, having received the word in much affliction, with joy of the Holy Ghost:

2 TIMOTHY 1:14 - That good thing which was committed unto thee keep by the Holy Ghost which dwelleth in us.

TITUS 3:5 - Not by works of righteousness which we have done, but according to his mercy he saved us, by the washing of regeneration, and renewing of the Holy Ghost;

HEBREWS 2:4 - God also bearing them witness, both with signs and wonders, and with divers miracles, and gifts of the Holy Ghost, according to his own will?

2 PETER 1:21 - For the prophecy came not in old time by the will of man: but holy men of God spake as they were moved by the Holy Ghost.

1 JOHN 3:24 - And he that keepeth his commandments dwelleth in him, and he in him. And hereby we know that he abideth in us, by the Spirit which he hath given us.

1 JOHN 5:6 - This is he that came by water and blood, even Jesus Christ; not by water only, but by water and blood. And it is the Spirit that beareth witness, because the Spirit is truth.

1 JOHN 2:20 - But ye have an unction from the Holy One, and ye know all things.

HONOR

EXODUS 20:12 - Honour thy father and thy mother: that thy days may be long upon the land which the LORD thy God giveth thee.

1 SAMUEL 2:30 - Wherefore the LORD God of Israel saith, I said indeed that thy house, and the house of thy father, should walk before me for ever: but now the LORD saith, Be it far from me; for them that honour me I will honour, and they that despise me shall be lightly esteemed.

1 KINGS 3:11-13 - And God said unto him, Because thou hast asked this thing, and hast not asked for thyself long life; neither hast asked riches for thyself, nor hast asked the life of thine enemies; but hast asked for thyself understanding to discern judgment; Behold, I have done according to thy words: lo, I have given thee a wise and an understanding heart; so that there was none like thee before thee, neither after thee shall any arise like unto thee. And I have also given thee that which thou hast not asked, both riches, and honour: so that there shall not be any among the kings like unto thee all thy days.

1 CHRONICLES 16:25,27 - For great is the LORD, and greatly to be praised: he also is to be feared above all gods. Glory and honour are in his presence; strength and gladness are in his place.

1 CHRONICLES 29:11-12 - Thine, O LORD, is the greatness, and the power, and the glory, and the victory, and the majesty: for all that is in the heaven and in the earth is thine; thine is the kingdom, O LORD, and thou art exalted as head above all. Both riches and honour come of thee, and thou reignest over all; and in thine hand is power and might; and in thine hand it is to make great, and to give strength unto all.

PSALMS 8:4-5 - What is man, that thou art mindful of him? and the son of man, that thou visitest him? For thou hast made him a little lower than the angels, and hast crowned him with glory and honour.

PSALMS 26:8 - LORD, I have loved the habitation of thy house, and the place where thine honour dwelleth.

PSALMS 37:34 - Wait on the LORD, and keep his way, and he shall exalt thee to inherit the land: when the wicked are cut off, thou shalt see it.

PSALMS 89:16-17 - In thy name shall they rejoice all the day: and in thy righteousness shall they be exalted. For thou art the glory of their strength: and in thy favour our horn shall be exalted.

PSALMS 91:14-15 - Because he hath set his love upon me, therefore will I deliver him: I will set him on high, because he hath known my name. He shall call upon me, and I will answer him: I will be with him in trouble; I will deliver him, and honour him.

PSALMS 112:5-9 - A good man showeth favour, and lendeth: he will guide his affairs with discretion. Surely he shall not be moved for ever: the righteous shall be in everlasting remembrance. He shall not be afraid of evil tidings: his heart is fixed, trusting in the LORD. His heart is established, he shall not be afraid, until he see his desire upon his enemies. He hath dispersed, he hath given to the poor; his righteousness endureth for ever; his horn shall be exalted with honour.

PROVERBS 3:13,16 - Happy is the man that findeth wisdom, and the man that getteth understanding. Length of days is in her right hand; and in her left hand riches and honour.

PROVERBS 4:7-8 - Wisdom is the principal thing; therefore get wisdom: and with all thy getting get understanding. Exalt her, and she shall promote thee: she shall bring thee to honour, when thou dost embrace her.

PROVERBS 11:16 - A gracious woman retaineth honour: and strong men retain riches.

PROVERBS 13:18 - Poverty and shame shall be to him that refuseth instruction: but he that regardeth reproof shall be honoured.

PROVERBS 14:28 - In the multitude of people is the king's honour: but in the want of people is the destruction of the prince.

PROVERBS 15:33 - The fear of the LORD is the instruction of wisdom; and before honour is humility.

PROVERBS 20:3 - It is an honour for a man to cease from strife: but every fool will be meddling.

PROVERBS 21:21 - He that followeth after righteousness and mercy findeth life, righteousness, and honour.

PROVERBS 22:4 - By humility and the fear of the LORD are riches, and honour, and life.

PROVERBS 27:18 - Whoso keepeth the fig tree shall eat the fruit thereof: so he that waiteth on his master shall be honoured.

PROVERBS 29:23 - A man's pride shall bring him low: but honour shall uphold the humble in spirit.

PROVERBS 31:10,25 - Who can find a virtuous woman? for her price is far above rubies. Strength and honour are her clothing; and she shall rejoice in time to come.

ECCLESIASTES 10:1 - Dead flies cause the ointment of the apothecary to send forth a stinking savour: so doth a little folly him that is in reputation for wisdom and honour.

MATTHEW 13:57 - And they were offended in him. But Jesus said unto them, A prophet is not without honour, save in his own country, and in his own house.

MATTHEW 23:12 - And whosoever shall exalt himself shall be abased; and he that shall humble himself shall be exalted.

JOHN 5:43-44 - I am come in my Father's name, and ye receive me not: if another shall come in his own name, him ye will receive. How can ye believe, which receive honour one of another, and seek not the honour that cometh from God only?

JOHN 12:26 - If any man serve me, let him follow me; and where I am, there shall also my servant be: if any man serve me, him will my Father honour.

ROMANS 2:10 - But glory, honour, and peace, to every man that worketh good, to the Jew first, and also to the Gentile:

ROMANS 12:10 - Be kindly affectioned one to another with brotherly love; in honour preferring one another;

PHILIPPIANS 2:3 - Let nothing be done through strife or vainglory; but in lowliness of mind let each esteem other better than themselves.

1 THESSALONIANS 5:12-13 - And we beseech you, brethren, to know them which labour among you, and are over you in the Lord, and admonish you; And to esteem them very highly in love for their work's sake. And be at peace among yourselves.

1 TIMOTHY 6:1 - Let as many servants as are under the yoke count their own masters worthy of all honour, that the name of God and his doctrine be not blasphemed.

2 TIMOTHY 2:21 - If a man therefore purge himself from these, he shall be a vessel unto honour, sanctified, and meet for the master's use, and prepared unto every good work.

JAMES 1:9 - Let the brother of low degree rejoice in that he is exalted:

1 PETER 1:7 - That the trial of your faith, being much more precious than of gold that perisheth, though it be tried with fire, might be found unto praise and honour and glory at the appearing of Jesus Christ:

1 PETER 2:17 - Honour all men. Love the brotherhood. Fear God. Honour the king.

1 PETER 3:7 - Likewise, ye husbands, dwell with them according to knowledge, giving honour unto the wife, as unto the weaker vessel, and as being heirs together of the grace of life; that your prayers be not hindered.

1 PETER 5:6 - Humble yourselves therefore under the mighty hand of God, that he may exalt you in due time:

HOPE

PSALMS 16:8-9 - I have set the LORD always before me: because he is at my right hand, I shall not be moved. Therefore my heart is glad, and my glory rejoiceth: my flesh also shall rest in hope.

PSALMS 19:9-10 - The fear of the LORD is clean, enduring for ever: the judgments of the LORD are true and righteous altogether. More to be desired are they than gold, yea, than much fine gold: sweeter also than honey and the honeycomb.

PSALMS 37:4 - Delight thyself also in the LORD; and he shall give thee the desires of thine heart.

PSALMS 38:15 - For in thee, O LORD, do I hope: thou wilt hear, O Lord my God.

PSALMS 42:5 - Why art thou cast down, O my soul? and why art thou disquieted in me? hope thou in God: for I shall yet praise him for the help of his countenance.

PSALMS 71:14 - But I will hope continually, and will yet praise thee more and more.

PSALMS 119:81 - My soul fainteth for thy salvation: but I hope in thy word.

PSALMS 145:18-19 - The LORD is nigh unto all them that call upon him, to all that call upon him in truth. He will fulfil the desire of them that fear him: he also will hear their cry, and will save them.

PSALMS 146:5 - Happy is he that hath the God of Jacob for his help, whose hope is in the LORD his God:

PROVERBS 10:28 - The hope of the righteous shall be gladness: but the expectation of the wicked shall perish.

PROVERBS 13:12 - Hope deferred maketh the heart sick: but when the desire cometh, it is a tree of life.

PROVERBS 13:19 - The desire accomplished is sweet to the soul: but it is abomination to fools to depart from evil.

PROVERBS 14:32 - The wicked is driven away in his wickedness: but the righteous hath hope in his death.

PROVERBS 29:18 - Where there is no vision, the people perish: but he that keepeth the law, happy is he.

JEREMIAH 17:17 - Be not a terror unto me: thou art my hope in the day of evil.

HABAKKUK 2:2-3 - For the vision is yet for an appointed time, but at the end it shall speak, and not lie: though it tarry, wait for it; because it will surely come, it will not tarry.

ROMANS 4:18 - Who against hope believed in hope, that he might become the father of many nations, according to that which was spoken, So shall thy seed be.

ROMANS 5:3-5 - And not only so, but we glory in tribulations also: knowing that tribulation worketh patience; And patience, experience; and experience, hope: And hope maketh not ashamed; because the love of God is shed abroad in our hearts by the Holy Ghost which is given unto us.

1 CORINTHIANS 9:10 - Or saith he it altogether for our sakes? For our sakes, no doubt, this is written: that he that ploweth should plow in hope; and that he that thresheth in hope should be partaker of his hope.

1 CORINTHIANS 13:13 - And now abideth faith, hope, charity, these three; but the greatest of these is charity.

1 CORINTHIANS 15:19 - If in this life only we have hope in Christ, we are of all men most miserable.

EPHESIANS 1:17-18 - That the God of our Lord Jesus Christ, the Father of glory, may give unto you the spirit of wisdom and revelation in the knowledge of him: The eyes of your understanding being enlightened; that ye may know what is the hope of his calling, and what the riches of the glory of his inheritance in the saints,

COLOSSIANS 1:3-5 - We give thanks to God and the Father of our Lord Jesus Christ, praying always for you, Since we heard of your faith in Christ Jesus, and of the love which ye have to all the saints, For the hope which is laid up for you in heaven, whereof ye heard before in the word of the truth of the gospel;

COLOSSIANS 1:27 - To whom God would make known what is the riches of the glory of this mystery among the Gentiles; which is Christ in you, the hope of glory:

EPHESIANS 2:12 - That at that time ye were without Christ, being aliens from the commonwealth of Israel, and strangers from the covenants of promise, having no hope, and without God in the world:

1 THESSALONIANS 4:13-14 - But I would not have you to be ignorant, brethren, concerning them which are asleep, that ye sorrow not, even as others which have no hope. For if we believe that Jesus died and rose again, even so them also which sleep in Jesus will God bring with him.

1 THESSALONIANS 5:8 - But let us, who are of the day, be sober, putting on the breastplate of faith and love; and for an helmet, the hope of salvation.

1 TIMOTHY 1:1 - Paul, an apostle of Jesus Christ by the commandment of God our Saviour, and Lord Jesus Christ, which is our hope;

TITUS 2:13 - Looking for that blessed hope, and the glorious appearing of the great God and our Saviour Jesus Christ;

HEBREWS 3:6 - But Christ as a son over his own house; whose house are we, if we hold fast the confidence and the rejoicing of the hope firm unto the end.

HEBREWS 6:11 - And we desire that every one of you do show the same diligence to the full assurance of hope unto the end:

HEBREWS 6:18-19 - That by two immutable things, in which it was impossible for God to lie, we might have a strong consolation, who have fled for refuge to lay hold upon the hope set before us: Which hope we have as an anchor of the soul, both sure and stedfast, and which entereth into that within the veil;

HEBREWS 11:1 - Now faith is the substance of things hoped for, the evidence of things not seen.

1 PETER 1:3 - Blessed be the God and Father of our Lord Jesus Christ, which according to his abundant mercy hath begotten us again unto a lively hope by the resurrection of Jesus Christ from the dead,

1 PETER 3:15 - But sanctify the Lord God in your hearts: and be ready always to give an answer to every man that asketh you a reason of the hope that is in you with meekness and fear:

1 JOHN 5:14-15 - And this is the confidence that we have in him, that, if we ask any thing according to his will, he heareth us: And if we know that he hear us, whatsoever we ask, we know that we have the petitions that we desired of him.

INTEGRITY OF GOD'S WORD

GENESIS 18:14 - Is any thing too hard for the LORD? At the time appointed I will return unto thee, according to the time of life, and Sarah shall have a son.

NUMBERS 11:23 - And the LORD said unto Moses, Is the LORD'S hand waxed short? thou shalt see now whether my word shall come to pass unto thee or not.

NUMBERS 23:19 - God is not a man, that he should lie; neither the son of man, that he should repent: hath he said, and shall he not do it? or hath he spoken, and shall he not make it good?

DEUTERONOMY 7:9 - Know therefore that the LORD thy God, he is God, the faithful God, which keepeth covenant and mercy with them that love him and keep his commandments to a thousand generations;

JOSHUA 21:45 - There failed not ought of any good thing which the LORD had spoken unto the house of Israel; all came to pass.

JUDGES 2:1 - And an angel of the LORD came up from Gilgal to Bochim, and said, I made you to go up out of Egypt, and have brought you unto the land which I sware unto your fathers; and I said, I will never break my covenant with you.

1 KINGS 8:56 - Blessed be the LORD, that hath given rest unto his people Israel, according to all that he promised: there hath not failed one word of all his good promise, which he promised by the hand of Moses his servant.

PSALMS 33:4,9 - For the word of the LORD is right; and all his works are done in truth. For he spake, and it was done; he commanded, and it stood fast.

PSALMS 33:11 - The counsel of the LORD standeth for ever, the thoughts of his heart to all generations.

PSALMS 89:34 - My covenant will I not break, nor alter the thing that is gone out of my lips.

PSALMS 93:5 - Thy testimonies are very sure: holiness becometh thine house, O LORD, for ever.

PSALMS 100:5 - For the LORD is good; his mercy is everlasting; and his truth endureth to all generations.

PSALMS 105:8 - He hath remembered his covenant for ever, the word which he commanded to a thousand generations.

PSALMS 105:19 - Until the time that his word came: the word of the LORD tried him.

PSALMS 111:5 - He hath given meat unto them that fear him: he will ever be mindful of his covenant.

PSALMS 111:7-8 - The works of his hands are verity and judgment; all his commandments are sure. They stand fast for ever and ever, and are done in truth and uprightness.

PSALMS 119:89-90 - For ever, O LORD, thy word is settled in heaven. Thy faithfulness is unto all generations: thou hast established the earth, and it abideth.

PSALMS 119:138 - Thy testimonies that thou hast commanded are righteous and very faithful.

PSALMS 119:160 - Thy word is true from the beginning: and every one of thy righteous judgments endureth for ever.

ISAIAH 14:24 - The LORD of hosts hath sworn, saying, Surely as I have thought, so shall it come to pass; and as I have purposed, so shall it stand:

ISAIAH 25:1 - O LORD, thou art my God; I will exalt thee, I will praise thy name; for thou hast done wonderful things; thy counsels of old are faithfulness and truth.

ISAIAH 46:9-11 - Remember the former things of old: for I am God, and there is none else; I am God, and there is none like me, Declaring the end from the beginning, and from ancient times the things that are not yet done, saying, My counsel shall stand, and I will do all my pleasure: Calling a ravenous bird from the east, the man that executeth my counsel from a far country: yea, I have spoken it, I will also bring it to pass; I have purposed it, I will also do it.

ISAIAH 55:10-11 - For as the rain cometh down, and the snow from heaven, and returneth not thither, but watereth the earth, and maketh it bring forth and bud, that it may give seed to the sower, and bread to the eater: So shall my word be that goeth forth out of my mouth: it shall not return unto me void, but it shall accomplish that which I please, and it shall prosper in the thing whereto I sent it.

JEREMIAH 1:12 - Then said the LORD unto me, Thou hast well seen: for I will hasten my word to perform it.

JEREMIAH 32:17 - Ah Lord GOD! behold, thou hast made the heaven and the earth by thy great power and stretched out arm, and there is nothing too hard for thee:

JEREMIAH 32:27 - Behold, I am the LORD, the God of all flesh: is there any thing too hard for me?

MATTHEW 5:18 - For verily I say unto you, Till heaven and earth pass, one jot or one tittle shall in no wise pass from the law, till all be fulfilled.

MATTHEW 19:26 - But Jesus beheld them, and said unto them, With men this is impossible; but with God all things are possible.

MATTHEW 24:35 - Heaven and earth shall pass away, but my words shall not pass away.

MARK 9:23 - Jesus said unto him, If thou canst believe, all things are possible to him that believeth.

LUKE 1:37 - For with God nothing shall be impossible.

LUKE 16:17 - And it is easier for heaven and earth to pass, than one tittle of the law to fail.

JOHN 17:17 - Sanctify them through thy truth: thy word is truth.

ROMANS 3:3-4 - For what if some did not believe? shall their unbelief make the faith of God without effect? God forbid: yea, let God be true, but every man a liar; as it is written, That thou mightest be justified in thy sayings, and mightest overcome when thou art judged.

ROMANS 4:16 - Therefore it is of faith, that it might be by grace; to the end the promise might be sure to all the seed; not to that only which is of the law, but to that also which is of the faith of Abraham; who is the father of us all,

2 CORINTHIANS 1:20 - For all the promises of God in him are yea, and in him Amen, unto the glory of God by us.

GALATIANS 3:29 - And if ye be Christ's, then are ye Abraham's seed, and heirs according to the promise.

ROMANS 2:11 - For there is no respect of persons with God.

TITUS 1:2 - In hope of eternal life, which God, that cannot lie, promised before the world began;

HEBREWS 6:17-18 - Wherein God, willing more abundantly to show unto the heirs of promise the immutability of his counsel, confirmed it by an oath: That by two immutable things, in which it was impossible for God to lie, we might have a strong consolation, who have fled for refuge to lay hold upon the hope set before us:

JAMES 1:17 - Every good gift and every perfect gift is from above, and cometh down from the Father of lights, with whom is no variableness, neither shadow of turning.

1 PETER 1:25 - But the word of the Lord endureth for ever. And this is the word which by the gospel is preached unto you.

2 PETER 1:4 - Whereby are given unto us exceeding great and precious promises: that by these ye might be partakers of the divine nature, having escaped the corruption that is in the world through lust.

2 PETER 3:9 - The Lord is not slack concerning his promise, as some men count slackness; but is longsuffering to us-ward, not willing that any should perish, but that all should come to repentance.

JOY

NEHEMIAH 8:10 - Then he said unto them, Go your way, eat the fat, and drink the sweet, and send portions unto them for whom nothing is prepared: for this day is holy unto our Lord: neither be ye sorry; for the joy of the LORD is your strength.

1 CHRONICLES 15:16 - And David spake to the chief of the Levites to appoint their brethren to be the singers with instruments of music, psalteries and harps and cymbals, sounding, by lifting up the voice with joy.

1 CHRONICLES 16:27 - Glory and honour are in his presence; strength and gladness are in his place.

2 CHRONICLES 6:41 - Now therefore arise, O LORD God, into thy resting place, thou, and the ark of thy strength: let thy priests, O LORD God, be clothed with salvation, and let thy saints rejoice in goodness.

PSALMS 4:7 - Thou hast put gladness in my heart, more than in the time that their corn and their wine increased.

PSALMS 5:11 - But let all those that put their trust in thee rejoice: let them ever shout for joy, because thou defendest them: let them also that love thy name be joyful in thee

PSALMS 16:11 - Thou wilt show me the path of life: in thy presence is fulness of joy; at thy right hand there are pleasures for evermore.

PSALMS 19:8 - The statutes of the LORD are right, rejoicing the heart: the commandment of the LORD is pure, enlightening the eyes.

PSALMS 30:5 - For his anger endureth but a moment; in his favour is life: weeping may endure for a night, but joy cometh in the morning.

PSALMS 31:7 - I will be glad and rejoice in thy mercy: for thou hast considered my trouble; thou hast known my soul in adversities;

PSALMS 32:11 - Be glad in the LORD, and rejoice, ye righteous: and shout for joy, all ye that are upright in heart.

PSALMS 35:9 - And my soul shall be joyful in the LORD: it shall rejoice in his salvation.

PSALMS 35:27 - Let them shout for joy, and be glad, that favour my righteous cause: yea, let them say continually, Let the LORD be magnified, which hath pleasure in the prosperity of his servant.

PSALMS 40:16 - Let all those that seek thee rejoice and be glad in thee: let such as love thy salvation say continually, The LORD be magnified.

PSALMS 43:4 - Then will I go unto the altar of God, unto God my exceeding joy: yea, upon the harp will I praise thee, O God my God.

PSALMS 64:10 - The righteous shall be glad in the LORD, and shall trust in him; and all the upright in heart shall glory.

PSALMS 66:1-2 - Make a joyful noise unto God, all ye lands: Sing forth the honour of his name: make his praise glorious.

PSALMS 67:4 - O let the nations be glad and sing for joy: for thou shalt judge the people righteously, and govern the nations upon earth. Selah.

PSALMS 70:4 - Let all those that seek thee rejoice and be glad in thee: and let such as love thy salvation say continually, Let God be magnified.

PSALMS 90:14 - O satisfy us early with thy mercy; that we may rejoice and be glad all our days.

PSALMS 92:4 - For thou, LORD, hast made me glad through thy work: I will triumph in the works of thy hands.

PSALMS 97:1 - The LORD reigneth; let the earth rejoice; let the multitude of isles be glad thereof.

PSALMS 100:1-2 - Make a joyful noise unto the LORD, all ye lands. Serve the LORD with gladness: come before his presence with singing.

PSALMS 104:31 - The glory of the LORD shall endure for ever: the LORD shall rejoice in his works.

PSALMS 104:34 - My meditation of him shall be sweet: I will be glad in the LORD.

PSALMS 105:3 - Glory ye in his holy name: let the heart of them rejoice that seek the LORD.

PSALMS 105:43 - And he brought forth his people with joy, and his chosen with gladness:

PSALMS 118:15 - The voice of rejoicing and salvation is in the tabernacles of the righteous: the right hand of the LORD doeth valiantly.

PSALMS 118:24 - This is the day which the LORD hath made; we will rejoice and be glad in it.

PSALMS 119:111 - Thy testimonies have I taken as an heritage for ever: for they are the rejoicing of my heart.

PSALMS 119:162 - I rejoice at thy word, as one that findeth great spoil.

PSALMS 126:5 - They that sow in tears shall reap in joy.

PSALMS 132:9 - Let thy priests be clothed with righteousness; and let thy saints shout for joy.

PSALMS 149:5 - Let the saints be joyful in glory: let them sing aloud upon their beds.

PROVERBS 5:18 - Let thy fountain be blessed: and rejoice with the wife of thy youth.

PROVERBS 10:28 - The hope of the righteous shall be gladness: but the expectation of the wicked shall perish.

PROVERBS 11:10 - When it goeth well with the righteous, the city rejoiceth: and when the wicked perish, there is shouting.

PROVERBS 12:20 - Deceit is in the heart of them that imagine evil: but to the counsellors of peace is joy.

PROVERBS 13:9 - The light of the righteous rejoiceth: but the lamp of the wicked shall be put out.

PROVERBS 15:13 - A merry heart maketh a cheerful countenance: but by sorrow of the heart the spirit is broken.

PROVERBS 15:15 - All the days of the afflicted are evil: but he that is of a merry heart hath a continual feast.

PROVERBS 15:23 - A man hath joy by the answer of his mouth: and a word spoken in due season, how good is it!

PROVERBS 15:30 - The light of the eyes rejoiceth the heart: and a good report maketh the bones fat.

PROVERBS 17:22 - A merry heart doeth good like a medicine: but a broken spirit drieth the bones.

PROVERBS 21:15 - It is joy to the just to do judgment: but destruction shall be to the workers of iniquity.

PROVERBS 23:24 - The father of the righteous shall greatly rejoice: and he that begetteth a wise child shall have joy of him.

PROVERBS 27:9 - Ointment and perfume rejoice the heart: so doth the sweetness of a man's friend by hearty counsel.

PROVERBS 28:12 - When righteous men do rejoice, there is great glory: but when the wicked rise, a man is hidden.

PROVERBS 29:2 - When the righteous are in authority, the people rejoice: but when the wicked beareth rule, the people mourn.

ISAIAH 12:3 - Therefore with joy shall ye draw water out of the wells of salvation.

ISAIAH 29:19 - The meek also shall increase their joy in the LORD, and the poor among men shall rejoice in the Holy One of Israel.

ISAIAH 35:10 - And the ransomed of the LORD shall return, and come to Zion with songs and everlasting joy upon their heads: they shall obtain joy and gladness, and sorrow and sighing shall flee away.

ISAIAH 51:11 - Therefore the redeemed of the LORD shall return, and come with singing unto Zion; and everlasting joy shall be upon their head: they shall obtain gladness and joy; and sorrow and mourning shall flee away.

ISAIAH 56:7 - Even them will I bring to my holy mountain, and make them joyful in my house of prayer: their burnt offerings and their sacrifices shall be accepted upon mine altar; for mine house shall be called an house of prayer for all people.

ISAIAH 61:10 - I will greatly rejoice in the LORD, my soul shall be joyful in my God; for he hath clothed me with the garments of salvation, he hath covered me with the robe of righteousness, as a bridegroom decketh himself with ornaments, and as a bride adorneth herself with her jewels.

ISAIAH 65:18 - But be ye glad and rejoice for ever in that which I create: for, behold, I create Jerusalem a rejoicing, and her people a joy.

JEREMIAH 15:16 - Thy words were found, and I did eat them; and thy word was unto me the joy and rejoicing of mine heart: for I am called by thy name, O LORD God of hosts.

JEREMIAH 32:41 - Yea, I will rejoice over them to do them good, and I will plant them in this land assuredly with my whole heart and with my whole soul.

MATTHEW 5:11-12 - Blessed are ye, when men shall revile you, and persecute you, and shall say all manner of evil against you falsely, for my sake. Rejoice, and be exceeding glad: for great is your reward in heaven: for so persecuted they the prophets which were before you.

LUKE 2:10-11 - And the angel said unto them, Fear not: for, behold, I bring you good tidings of great joy, which shall be to all people. For unto you is born this day in the city of David a Saviour, which is Christ the Lord.

LUKE 10:20-21 - Notwithstanding in this rejoice not, that the spirits are subject unto you; but rather rejoice, because your names are written in heaven. In that hour Jesus rejoiced in spirit, and said, I thank thee, O Father, Lord of heaven and earth, that thou hast hid these things from the wise and prudent, and hast revealed them unto babes: even so, Father; for so it seemed good in thy sight.

LUKE 15:7 - I say unto you, that likewise joy shall be in heaven over one sinner that repenteth, more than over ninety and nine just persons, which need no repentance.

JOHN 4:36 - And he that reapeth receiveth wages, and gathereth fruit unto life eternal: that both he that soweth and he that reapeth may rejoice together.

JOHN 15:11 - These things have I spoken unto you, that my joy might remain in you, and that your joy might be full.

JOHN 16:22 - And ye now therefore have sorrow: but I will see you again, and your heart shall rejoice, and your joy no man taketh from you.

JOHN 16:24 - Hitherto have ye asked nothing in my name: ask, and ye shall receive, that your joy may be full.

JOHN 17:13 - And now come I to thee; and these things I speak in the world, that they might have my joy fulfilled in themselves.

ACTS 2:46-47 - And they, continuing daily with one accord in the temple, and breaking bread from house to house, did eat their meat with gladness and singleness of heart, Praising God, and having favour with all the people. And the Lord added to the church daily such as should be saved.

ACTS 5:41- And they departed from the presence of the council, rejoicing that they were counted worthy to suffer shame for his name.

ACTS 8:6-8 - And the people with one accord gave heed unto those things which Philip spake, hearing and seeing the miracles which he did. For unclean spirits, crying with loud voice, came out of many that were possessed with them: and many taken with palsies, and that were lame, were healed. And there was great joy in that city.

ACTS 15:3 - And being brought on their way by the church, they passed through Phenice and Samaria, declaring the conversion of the Gentiles: and they caused great joy unto all the brethren.

ACTS 20:24 - But none of these things move me, neither count I my life dear unto myself, so that I might finish my course with joy, and the ministry, which I have received of the Lord Jesus, to testify the gospel of the grace of God.

ROMANS 12:15 - Rejoice with them that do rejoice, and weep with them that weep.

ROMANS 14:17 - For the kingdom of God is not meat and drink; but righteousness, and peace, and joy in the Holy Ghost.

ROMANS 15:13 - Now the God of hope fill you with all joy and peace in believing, that ye may abound in hope, through the power of the Holy Ghost.

1 CORINTHIANS 13:4,6 - Charity suffereth long, and is kind; charity envieth not; charity vaunteth not itself, is not puffed up, Rejoiceth not in iniquity, but rejoiceth in the truth;

GALATIANS 5:22 - But the fruit of the Spirit is love, joy, peace, longsuffering, gentleness, goodness, faith,

PHILIPPIANS 1:3-4 - I thank my God upon every remembrance of you, Always in every prayer of mine for you all making request with joy,

PHILIPPIANS 4:4 - Rejoice in the Lord alway: and again I say, Rejoice.

1 THESSALONIANS 1:6 - And ye became followers of us, and of the Lord, having received the word in much affliction, with joy of the Holy Ghost:

1 THESSALONIANS 5:16 - Rejoice evermore.

HEBREWS 12:2 - Looking unto Jesus the author and finisher of our faith; who for the joy that was set before him endured the cross, despising the shame, and is set down at the right hand of the throne of God.

JAMES 1:2-4 - My brethren, count it all joy when ye fall into divers temptations; Knowing this, that the trying of your faith worketh patience. But let patience have her perfect work, that ye may be perfect and entire, wanting nothing.

JAMES 5:13 - Is any among you afflicted? let him pray. Is any merry? let him sing psalms.

1 PETER 4:12-13 - Beloved, think it not strange concerning the fiery trial which is to try you, as though some strange thing happened unto you: But rejoice, inasmuch as ye are partakers of Christ's sufferings; that, when his glory shall be revealed, ye may be glad also with exceeding joy.

1 JOHN 1:4 - And these things write we unto you, that your joy may be full.

3 JOHN 1:4 - I have no greater joy than to hear that my children walk in truth.

REVELATION 19:7 - Let us be glad and rejoice, and give honour to him: for the marriage of the Lamb is come, and his wife hath made herself ready.

LONELINESS

GENESIS 2:18 - And the LORD God said, It is not good that the man should be alone; I will make him an help meet for him.

DEUTERONOMY 31:6 - Be strong and of a good courage, fear not, nor be afraid of them: for the LORD thy God, he it is that doth go with thee; he will not fail thee, nor forsake thee.

1 SAMUEL 12:22 - For the LORD will not forsake his people for his great name's sake: because it hath pleased the LORD to make you his people.

PSALMS 27:10 - When my father and my mother forsake me, then the LORD will take me up.

PSALMS 37:3-5 - Trust in the LORD, and do good; so shalt thou dwell in the land, and verily thou shalt be fed. Delight thyself also in the LORD; and he shall give thee the desires of thine heart. Commit thy way unto the LORD; trust also in him; and he shall bring it to pass.

PSALMS 68:6 - God setteth the solitary in families: he bringeth out those which are bound with chains: but the rebellious dwell in a dry land.

PSALMS 147:2-3 - The LORD doth build up Jerusalem: he gathereth together the outcasts of Israel. He healeth the broken in heart, and bindeth up their wounds.

ISAIAH 41:10 - Fear thou not; for I am with thee: be not dismayed; for I am thy God: I will strengthen thee; yea, I will help thee; yea, I will uphold thee with the right hand of my righteousness.

ISAIAH 54:4-5 - Fear not; for thou shalt not be ashamed: neither be thou confounded; for thou shalt not be put to shame: for thou shalt forget the shame of thy youth, and shalt not remember the reproach of thy widowhood any more. For thy Maker is thine husband; the LORD of hosts is his name; and thy Redeemer the Holy One of Israel; The God of the whole earth shall he be called.

MATTHEW 28:19-20 - Go ye therefore, and teach all nations, baptizing them in the name of the Father, and of the Son, and of the Holy Ghost: Teaching them to observe all things whatsoever I have commanded you: and, lo, I am with you alway, even unto the end of the world. Amen.

JOHN 14:2-3 - In my Father's house are many mansions: if it were not so, I would have told you. I go to prepare a place for you. And if I go and prepare a place for you, I will come again, and receive you unto myself; that where I am, there ye may be also.

JOHN 14:16-18 - And I will pray the Father, and he shall give you another Comforter, that he may abide with you for ever; Even the Spirit of truth; whom the world cannot receive, because it seeth him not, neither knoweth him: but ye know him; for he dwelleth with you, and shall be in you.

JOHN 16:7 - Nevertheless I tell you the truth; It is expedient for you that I go away: for if I go not away, the Comforter will not come unto you; but if I depart, I will send him unto you.

JOHN 16:13 - Howbeit when he, the Spirit of truth, is come, he will guide you into all truth: for he shall not speak of himself; but whatsoever he shall hear, that shall he speak: and he will show you things to come.

PHILIPPIANS 4:11 - Not that I speak in respect of want: for I have learned, in whatsoever state I am, therewith to be content.

1 THESSALONIANS 5:11 - Wherefore comfort yourselves together, and edify one another, even as also ye do.

1 THESSALONIANS 5:16 - Rejoice evermore.

1 THESSALONIANS 5:17 - Pray without ceasing.

HEBREWS 10:24-25 - And let us consider one another to provoke unto love and to good works: Not forsaking the assembling of ourselves together, as the manner of some is; but exhorting one another: and so much the more, as ye see the day approaching.

LONG LIFE

EXODUS 20:12 - Honour thy father and thy mother: that thy days may be long upon the land which the LORD thy God giveth thee.

EXODUS 23:25-26 - And ye shall serve the LORD your God, and he shall bless thy bread, and thy water; and I will take sickness away from the midst of thee. There shall nothing cast their young, nor be barren, in thy land: the number of thy days I will fulfil.

DEUTERONOMY 5:16 - Honour thy father and thy mother, as the LORD thy God hath commanded thee; that thy days may be prolonged, and that it may go well with thee, in the land which the LORD thy God giveth thee.

DEUTERONOMY 5:33 - Ye shall walk in all the ways which the LORD your God hath commanded you, that ye may live, and that it may be well with you, and that ye may prolong your days in the land which ye shall possess.

DEUTERONOMY 11:18-21 - Therefore shall ye lay up these my words in your heart and in your soul, and bind them for a sign upon your hand, that they may be as frontlets between your eyes. And ye shall teach them your children, speaking of them when thou sittest in thine house, and when thou walkest by the way, when thou liest down, and when thou risest up. And thou shalt write them upon the door posts of thine house, and upon thy gates: That your days may be multiplied, and the days of your children, in the land which the LORD sware unto your fathers to give them, as the days of heaven upon the earth.

DEUTERONOMY 25:15 - But thou shalt have a perfect and just weight, a perfect and just measure shalt thou have: that thy days may be lengthened in the land which the LORD thy God giveth thee.

DEUTERONOMY 30:19-20 - I call heaven and earth to record this day against you, that I have set before you life and death, blessing and cursing: therefore choose life, that both thou and thy seed may live: That thou mayest love the LORD thy God, and that thou mayest obey his voice, and that thou mayest cleave unto him: for he is thy life, and the length of thy days: that thou mayest dwell in the land which the LORD sware unto thy fathers, to Abraham, to Isaac, and to Jacob, to give them.

DEUTERONOMY 32:46-47 - And he said unto them, Set your hearts unto all the words which I testify among you this day, which ye shall command your children to observe to do, all the words of this law. For it is not a vain thing for you; because it is your life: and through this thing ye shall prolong your days in the land, whither ye go over Jordan to possess it.

PSALMS 34:12-14 - What man is he that desireth life, and loveth many days, that he may see good? Keep thy tongue from evil, and thy lips from speaking guile. Depart from evil, and do good; seek peace, and pursue it.

PSALMS 36:9 - For with thee is the fountain of life: in thy light shall we see light.

PSALMS 49:15 - But God will redeem my soul from the power of the grave: for he shall receive me. Selah.

PSALMS 61:6 - Thou wilt prolong the king's life: and his years as many generations.

PSALMS 91:14-16 - Because he hath set his love upon me, therefore will I deliver him: I will set him on high, because he hath known my name. He shall call upon me, and I will answer him: I will be with him in trouble; I will deliver him, and honour him. With long life will I satisfy him, and show him my salvation.

PSALMS 102:24 - I said, O my God, take me not away in the midst of my days: thy years are throughout all generations.

PSALMS 118:17-18 - I shall not die, but live, and declare the works of the LORD. The LORD hath chastened me sore: but he hath not given me over unto death.

PSALMS 119:17 - Deal bountifully with thy servant, that I may live, and keep thy word.

PSALMS 128:1,6 - Blessed is every one that feareth the LORD; that walketh in his ways. Yea, thou shalt see thy children's children, and peace upon Israel.

PROVERBS 3:1-2 - My son, forget not my law; but let thine heart keep my commandments: For length of days, and long life, and peace, shall they add to thee.

PROVERBS 3:13,16 - Happy is the man that findeth wisdom, and the man that getteth understanding. For the merchandise of it is better than the merchandise of silver, and the gain thereof than fine gold.

PROVERBS 4:10 - Hear, O my son, and receive my sayings; and the years of thy life shall be many.

PROVERBS 7:2 - Keep my commandments, and live; and my law as the apple of thine eye.

PROVERBS 9:6 - Forsake the foolish, and live; and go in the way of understanding.

PROVERBS 9:10-11 - For by me thy days shall be multiplied, and the years of thy life shall be increased. If thou be wise, thou shalt be wise for thyself: but if thou scornest, thou alone shalt bear it.

PROVERBS 10:11 - The mouth of a righteous man is a well of life: but violence covereth the mouth of the wicked.

PROVERBS 10:16 - The labour of the righteous tendeth to life: the fruit of the wicked to sin.

PROVERBS 10:27 - The fear of the LORD prolongeth days: but the years of the wicked shall be shortened.

PROVERBS 12:28 - In the way of righteousness is life; and in the pathway thereof there is no death.

PROVERBS 13:3 - He that keepeth his mouth keepeth his life: but he that openeth wide his lips shall have destruction.

PROVERBS 13:14 - The law of the wise is a fountain of life, to depart from the snares of death.

PROVERBS 15:4 - A wholesome tongue is a tree of life: but perverseness therein is a breach in the spirit.

PROVERBS 28:16 - The prince that wanteth understanding is also a great oppressor: but he that hateth covetousness shall prolong his days.

ECCLESIASTES 7:12 - For wisdom is a defence, and money is a defence: but the excellency of knowledge is, that wisdom giveth life to them that have it.

ECCLESIASTES 7:17 - Be not over much wicked, neither be thou foolish: why shouldest thou die before thy time?

ROMANS 8:6 - For to be carnally minded is death; but to be spiritually minded is life and peace.

1 CORINTHIANS 3:21-22 - Therefore let no man glory in men. For all things are yours; Whether Paul, or Apollos, or Cephas, or the world, or life, or death, or things present, or things to come; all are yours;

EPHESIANS 6:1-3 - Children, obey your parents in the Lord: for this is right. Honour thy father and mother; which is the first commandment with promise; That it may be well with thee, and thou mayest live long on the earth.

1 PETER 3:10-11 - For he that will love life, and see good days, let him refrain his tongue from evil, and his lips that they speak no guile: Let him eschew evil, and do good; let him seek peace, and ensue it.

LOVE
DEFINED

1 CORINTHIANS 13:4-8 - Charity suffereth long, and is kind; charity envieth not; charity vaunteth not itself, is not puffed up, Doth not behave itself unseemly, seeketh not her own, is not easily provoked, thinketh no evil; Rejoiceth not in iniquity, but rejoiceth in the truth; Beareth all things, believeth all things, hopeth all things, endureth all things. Charity never faileth: but whether there be prophecies, they shall fail; whether there be tongues, they shall cease; whether there be knowledge, it shall vanish away.

ROMANS 5:5 - And hope maketh not ashamed; because the love of God is shed abroad in our hearts by the Holy Ghost which is given unto us.

GOD'S LOVE

JEREMIAH 31:3 - The LORD hath appeared of old unto me, saying, Yea, I have loved thee with an everlasting love: therefore with lovingkindness have I drawn thee.

JOHN 3:16 - For God so loved the world, that he gave his only begotten Son, that whosoever believeth in him should not perish, but have everlasting life.

JOHN 16:27 - For the Father himself loveth you, because ye have loved me, and have believed that I came out from God.

ROMANS 5:8 - But God commendeth his love toward us, in that, while we were yet sinners, Christ died for us.

1 JOHN 4:8-10,16,19 - He that loveth not knoweth not God; for God is love. In this was manifested the love of God toward us, because that God sent his only begotten Son into the world, that we might live through him. Herein is love, not that we loved God, but that he loved us, and sent his Son to be the propitiation for our sins. And we have known and believed the love that God hath to us. God is love; and he that dwelleth in love dwelleth in God, and God in him. We love him, because he first loved us.

DEUTERONOMY 10:12 - And now, Israel, what doth the LORD thy God require of thee, but to fear the LORD thy God, to walk in all his ways, and to love him, and to serve the LORD thy God with all thy heart and with all thy soul,

MATTHEW 10:37 - He that loveth father or mother more than me is not worthy of me: and he that loveth son or daughter more than me is not worthy of me.

MATTHEW 22:37 - Jesus said unto him, Thou shalt love the Lord thy God with all thy heart, and with all thy soul, and with all thy mind.

JOHN 14:21 - He that hath my commandments, and keepeth them, he it is that loveth me: and he that loveth me shall be loved of my Father, and I will love him, and will manifest myself to him.

JOHN 17:26 And I have declared unto them thy name, and will declare it: that the love wherewith thou hast loved me may be in them, and I in them.

OUR LOVE TOWARD OTHERS

LUKE 6:31-32,35 - And as ye would that men should do to you, do ye also to them likewise. For if ye love them which love you, what thank have ye? for sinners also love those that love them. But love ye your enemies, and do good, and lend, hoping for nothing again; and your reward shall be great, and ye shall be the children of the Highest: for he is kind unto the unthankful and to the evil.

JOHN 13:34-35 - A new commandment I give unto you, That ye love one another; as I have loved you, that ye also love one another. By this shall all men know that ye are my disciples, if ye have love one to another.

JOHN 15:12 - This is my commandment, That ye love one another, as I have loved you.

ROMANS 13:8,10 - Owe no man any thing, but to love one another: for he that loveth another hath fulfilled the law.

1 CORINTHIANS 16:14 - Let all your things be done with charity.

2 CORINTHIANS 5:14 - For the love of Christ constraineth us; because we thus judge, that if one died for all, then were all dead:

GALATIANS 5:6 - For in Jesus Christ neither circumcision availeth any thing, nor uncircumcision; but faith which worketh by love.

GALATIANS 5:14 - For all the law is fulfilled in one word, even in this; Thou shalt love thy neighbour as thyself.

EPHESIANS 5:1-2 - Be ye therefore followers of God, as dear children; And walk in love, as Christ also hath loved us, and hath given himself for us an offering and a sacrifice to God for a sweetsmelling savour.

COLOSSIANS 3:14 - And above all these things put on charity, which is the bond of perfectness.

1 PETER 1:22 - Seeing ye have purified your souls in obeying the truth through the Spirit unto unfeigned love of the brethren, see that ye love one another with a pure heart fervently:

1 PETER 3:8-9 - Finally, be ye all of one mind, having compassion one of another, love as brethren, be pitiful, be courteous: Not rendering evil for evil, or railing for railing: but contrariwise blessing; knowing that ye are thereunto called, that ye should inherit a blessing.

1 PETER 4:8 - And above all things have fervent charity among yourselves: for charity shall cover the multitude of sins.

1 JOHN 3:11,14 - For this is the message that ye heard from the beginning, that we should love one another. We know that we have passed from death unto life, because we love the brethren. He that loveth not his brother abideth in death.

1 JOHN 3:16-18 - Hereby perceive we the love of God, because he laid down his life for us: and we ought to lay down our lives for the brethren. But whoso hath this world's good, and seeth his brother have need, and shutteth up his bowels of compassion from him, how dwelleth the love of God in him? My little children, let us not love in word, neither in tongue; but in deed and in truth.

1 JOHN 3:23 - And this is his commandment, That we should believe on the name of his Son Jesus Christ, and love one another, as he gave us commandment.

1 JOHN 4:7 - Beloved, let us love one another: for love is of God; and every one that loveth is born of God, and knoweth God.

1 JOHN 4:11 - Beloved, if God so loved us, we ought also to love one another.

1 JOHN 4:20-21 - If a man say, I love God, and hateth his brother, he is a liar: for he that loveth not his brother whom he hath seen, how can he love God whom he hath not seen? And this commandment have we from him, That he who loveth God love his brother also.

MARRIAGE

GENESIS 2:18,21-24 - And the LORD God said, It is not good that the man should be alone; I will make him an help meet for him. And the LORD God caused a deep sleep to fall upon Adam, and he slept: and he took one of his ribs, and closed up the flesh instead thereof; And the rib, which the LORD God had taken from man, made he a woman, and brought her unto the man. And Adam said, This is now bone of my bones, and flesh of my flesh: she shall be called Woman, because she was taken out of Man. Therefore shall a man leave his father and his mother, and shall cleave unto his wife: and they shall be one flesh.

PROVERBS 5:18-19 - Let thy fountain be blessed: and rejoice with the wife of thy youth. Let her be as the loving hind and pleasant roe; let her breasts satisfy thee at all times; and be thou ravished always with her love.

PROVERBS 18:22 - Whoso findeth a wife findeth a good thing, and obtaineth favour of the LORD.

PROVERBS 19:14 - House and riches are the inheritance of fathers: and a prudent wife is from the LORD.

PROVERBS 31:10-12,26-28 - Who can find a virtuous woman? for her price is far above rubies. The heart of her husband doth safely trust in her, so that he shall have no need of spoil. She will do him good and not evil all the days of her life. She openeth her mouth with wisdom; and in her tongue is the law of kindness. She looketh well to the ways of her household, and eateth not the bread of idleness. Her children arise up, and call her blessed; her husband also, and he praiseth her.

MATTHEW 19:5-6 - And said, For this cause shall a man leave father and mother, and shall cleave to his wife: and they twain shall be one flesh? Wherefore they are no more twain, but one flesh. What therefore God hath joined together, let not man put asunder.

ROMANS 15:5-6 - Now the God of patience and consolation grant you to be likeminded one toward another according to Christ Jesus: That ye may with one mind and one mouth glorify God, even the Father of our Lord Jesus Christ.

1 CORINTHIANS 7:3-5 - Let the husband render unto the wife due benevolence: and likewise also the wife unto the husband. The wife hath not power of her own body, but the husband: and likewise also the husband hath not power of his own body, but the wife.

1 CORINTHIANS 7:10-11 - And unto the married I command, yet not I, but the Lord, Let not the wife depart from her husband: But and if she depart, let her remain unmarried, or be reconciled to her husband: and let not the husband put away his wife.

1 CORINTHIANS 7:12-16 - But to the rest speak I, not the Lord: If any brother hath a wife that believeth not, and she be pleased to dwell with him, let him not put her away. And the woman which hath an husband that believeth not, and if he be pleased to dwell with her,

let her not leave him. For the unbelieving husband is sanctified by the wife, and the unbelieving wife is sanctified by the husband: else were your children unclean; but now are they holy. But if the unbelieving depart, let him depart. A brother or a sister is not under bondage in such cases: but God hath called us to peace. For what knowest thou, O wife, whether thou shalt save thy husband? or how knowest thou, O man, whether thou shalt save thy wife?

1 CORINTHIANS 7:27-28 - Art thou bound unto a wife? seek not to be loosed. Art thou loosed from a wife? seek not a wife. But and if thou marry, thou hast not sinned; and if a virgin marry, she hath not sinned. Nevertheless such shall have trouble in the flesh: but I spare you.

1 CORINTHIANS 7:39-40 - The wife is bound by the law as long as her husband liveth; but if her husband be dead, she is at liberty to be married to whom she will; only in the Lord. But she is happier if she so abide, after my judgment: and I think also that I have the Spirit of God.

1 CORINTHIANS 13:4-8 - Charity suffereth long, and is kind; charity envieth not; charity vaunteth not itself, is not puffed up, Doth not behave itself unseemly, seeketh not her own, is not easily provoked, thinketh no evil; Rejoiceth not in iniquity, but rejoiceth in the truth; Beareth all things, believeth all things, hopeth all things, endureth all things. Charity never faileth: but whether there be prophecies, they shall fail; whether there be tongues, they shall cease; whether there be knowledge, it shall vanish away.

EPHESIANS 4:29-32 - Let no corrupt communication proceed out of your mouth, but that which is good to the use of edifying, that it may minister grace unto the hearers. And grieve not the holy Spirit of God, whereby ye are sealed unto the day of redemption. Let all bitterness, and wrath, and anger, and clamour, and evil speaking, be put away from you, with all malice: And be ye kind one to another, tenderhearted, forgiving one another, even as God for Christ's sake hath forgiven you.

EPHESIANS 5:22-33 - Wives, submit yourselves unto your own husbands, as unto the Lord. For the husband is the head of the wife, even as Christ is the head of the church: and he is the saviour of the body. Therefore as the church is subject unto Christ, so let the wives be to their own husbands in every thing. Husbands, love your wives, even as Christ also loved the church, and gave himself for it; That he might sanctify and cleanse it with the washing of water by the word, That he might present it to himself a glorious church, not having spot, or wrinkle, or any such thing; but that it should be holy and without blemish. So ought men to love their wives as their own bodies. He that loveth his wife loveth himself. For no man ever yet hated his own flesh; but nourisheth and cherisheth it, even as the Lord the church: For we are members of his body, of his flesh, and of his bones. For this cause shall a man leave his father and mother, and shall be joined unto his wife, and they two shall be one flesh. This is a great mystery: but I speak concerning Christ and the church. Nevertheless let every one of you in particular so love his wife even as himself; and the wife see that she reverence her husband.

PHILIPPIANS 1:6 - Being confident of this very thing, that he which hath begun a good work in you will perform it until the day of Jesus Christ:

PHILIPPIANS 1:27 - Only let your conversation be as it becometh the gospel of Christ: that whether I come and see you, or else be absent, I may hear of your affairs, that ye stand fast in one spirit, with one mind striving together for the faith of the gospel;

COLOSSIANS 3:18-19 - Wives, submit yourselves unto your own husbands, as it is fit in the Lord. Husbands, love your wives, and be not bitter against them.

TITUS 2:3-5 - The aged women likewise, that they be in behaviour as becometh holiness, not false accusers, not given to much wine, teachers of good things; That they may teach the young women to be sober, to love their husbands, to love their children, To be discreet, chaste, keepers at home, good, obedient to their own husbands, that the word of God be not blasphemed.

1 PETER 3:1-7 - Likewise, ye wives, be in subjection to your own husbands; that, if any obey not the word, they also may without the word be won by the conversation of the wives; While they behold your chaste conversation coupled with fear. Whose adorning let it not be that outward adorning of plaiting the hair, and of wearing of gold, or of putting on of apparel; But let it be the hidden man of the heart, in that which is not corruptible, even the ornament of a meek and quiet spirit, which is in the sight of God of great price. For after this manner in the old time the holy women also, who trusted in God, adorned themselves, being in subjection unto their own husbands: Even as Sara obeyed Abraham, calling him

lord: whose daughters ye are, as long as ye do well, and are not afraid with any amazement. Likewise, ye husbands, dwell with them according to knowledge, giving honour unto the wife, as unto the weaker vessel, and as being heirs together of the grace of life; that your prayers be not hindered.

PATIENCE

PSALMS 25:2-3 - O my God, I trust in thee: let me not be ashamed, let not mine enemies triumph over me. Yea, let none that wait on thee be ashamed: let them be ashamed which transgress without cause.

PSALMS 25:21 - Let integrity and uprightness preserve me; for I wait on thee.

PSALMS 27:14 - Wait on the LORD: be of good courage, and he shall strengthen thine heart: wait, I say, on the LORD.

PSALMS 33:20 - Our soul waiteth for the LORD: he is our help and our shield.

PSALMS 37:7-9 - Rest in the LORD, and wait patiently for him: fret not thyself because of him who prospereth in his way, because of the man who bringeth wicked devices to pass. Cease from anger, and forsake wrath: fret not thyself in any wise to do evil. For evildoers shall be cut off: but those that wait upon the LORD, they shall inherit the earth.

PSALMS 37:34 - Wait on the LORD, and keep his way, and he shall exalt thee to inherit the land: when the wicked are cut off, thou shalt see it.

PSALMS 62:1-2 - Truly my soul waiteth upon God: from him cometh my salvation. He only is my rock and my salvation; he is my defence; I shall not be greatly moved.

PSALMS 62:5 - My soul, wait thou only upon God; for my expectation is from him.

PSALMS 130:5-6 - I wait for the LORD, my soul doth wait, and in his word do I hope. My soul waiteth for the Lord more than they that watch for the morning: I say, more than they that watch for the morning.

ECCLESIASTES 7:8 - Better is the end of a thing than the beginning thereof: and the patient in spirit is better than the proud in spirit.

ISAIAH 28:16 - Therefore thus saith the Lord GOD, Behold, I lay in Zion for a foundation a stone, a tried stone, a precious corner stone, a sure foundation: he that believeth shall not make haste.

ISAIAH 40:31 - But they that wait upon the LORD shall renew their strength; they shall mount up with wings as eagles; they shall run, and not be weary; and they shall walk, and not faint.

ISAIAH 64:4 - For since the beginning of the world men have not heard, nor perceived by the ear, neither hath the eye seen, O God, beside thee, what he hath prepared for him that waiteth for him.

LAMENTATIONS 3:25 - The LORD is good unto them that wait for him, to the soul that seeketh him.

LUKE 8:15 - But that on the good ground are they, which in an honest and good heart, having heard the word, keep it, and bring forth fruit with patience.

LUKE 21:19 - In your patience possess ye your souls.

ROMANS 2:7 - To them who by patient continuance in well doing seek for glory and honour and immortality, eternal life:

ROMANS 5:3-4 - And not only so, but we glory in tribulations also: knowing that tribulation worketh patience; And patience, experience; and experience, hope:

ROMANS 8:25 - But if we hope for that we see not, then do we with patience wait for it.

ROMANS 12:12 - Rejoicing in hope; patient in tribulation; continuing instant in prayer;

ROMANS 15:4 - For whatsoever things were written aforetime were written for our learning, that we through patience and comfort of the scriptures might have hope.

GALATIANS 5:22-23 - But the fruit of the Spirit is love, joy, peace, longsuffering, gentleness, goodness, faith, Meekness, temperance: against such there is no law.

EPHESIANS 4:1-3 - I therefore, the prisoner of the Lord, beseech you that ye walk worthy of the vocation wherewith ye are called, With all lowliness and meekness, with longsuffering, forbearing one another in love; Endeavouring to keep the unity of the Spirit in the bond of peace.

COLOSSIANS 3:12 - Put on therefore, as the elect of God, holy and beloved, bowels of mercies, kindness, humbleness of mind, meekness, longsuffering;

1 THESSALONIANS 5:14 - Now we exhort you, brethren, warn them that are unruly, comfort the feeble-minded, support the weak, be patient toward all men.

2 THESSALONIANS 1:3-4 - We are bound to thank God always for you, brethren, as it is meet, because that your faith groweth exceedingly, and the charity of every one of you all toward each other aboundeth; So that we ourselves glory in you in the churches of God for your patience and faith in all your persecutions and tribulations that ye endure:

2 THESSALONIANS 3:5 - And the Lord direct your hearts into the love of God, and into the patient waiting for Christ.

TITUS 2:2 - That the aged men be sober, grave, temperate, sound in faith, in charity, in patience.

HEBREWS 6:11-12 - And we desire that every one of you do show the same diligence to the full assurance of hope unto the end: That ye be not slothful, but followers of them who through faith and patience inherit the promises.

HEBREWS 10:35-36 - Cast not away therefore your confidence, which hath great recompense of reward. For ye have need of patience, that, after ye have done the will of God, ye might receive the promise.

HEBREWS 12:1-2 - Wherefore seeing we also are compassed about with so great a cloud of witnesses, let us lay aside every weight, and the sin which doth so easily beset us, and let us run with patience the race that is set before us, Looking unto Jesus the author and finisher of our faith; who for the joy that was set before him endured the cross, despising the shame, and is set down at the right hand of the throne of God.

JAMES 1:2-4 - My brethren, count it all joy when ye fall into divers temptations; Knowing this, that the trying of your faith worketh patience. But let patience have her perfect work, that ye may be perfect and entire, wanting nothing.

JAMES 5:7-8 - Be patient therefore, brethren, unto the coming of the Lord. Behold, the husbandman waiteth for the precious fruit of the earth, and hath long patience for it, until he receive the early and latter rain. Be ye also patient; stablish your hearts: for the coming of the Lord draweth nigh.

1 PETER 1:5-8 - Who are kept by the power of God through faith unto salvation ready to be revealed in the last time. Wherein ye greatly rejoice, though now for a season, if need be, ye are in heaviness through manifold temptations: That the trial of your faith, being much more precious than of gold that perisheth, though it be tried with fire, might be found unto praise and honour and glory at the appearing of Jesus Christ: Whom having not seen, ye love; in whom, though now ye see him not, yet believing, ye rejoice with joy unspeakable and full of glory:

PEACE

LEVITICUS 26:3,6 - If ye walk in my statutes, and keep my commandments, and do them; And I will give peace in the land, and ye shall lie down, and none shall make you afraid: and I will rid evil beasts out of the land, neither shall the sword go through your land.

PSALMS 4:8 - I will both lay me down in peace, and sleep: for thou, LORD, only makest me dwell in safety.

PSALMS 29:11 - The LORD will give strength unto his people; the LORD will bless his people with peace.

PSALMS 37:11 - But the meek shall inherit the earth; and shall delight themselves in the abundance of peace.

PSALMS 37:37 - Mark the perfect man, and behold the upright: for the end of that man is peace.

PSALMS 71:1 - In thee, O LORD, do I put my trust: let me never be put to confusion.

PSALMS 85:8 - I will hear what God the LORD will speak: for he will speak peace unto his people, and to his saints: but let them not turn again to folly.

PSALMS 119:165 - Great peace have they which love thy law: and nothing shall offend them.

PSALMS 147:12-14 - Praise the LORD, O Jerusalem; praise thy God, O Zion. For he hath strengthened the bars of thy gates; he hath blessed thy children within thee. He maketh peace in thy borders, and filleth thee with the finest of the wheat.

PROVERBS 3:1-2 - My son, forget not my law; but let thine heart keep my commandments: For length of days, and long life, and peace, shall they add to thee.

PROVERBS 3:13,17 - Happy is the man that findeth wisdom, and the man that getteth understanding. Her ways are ways of pleasantness, and all her paths are peace.

PROVERBS 16:7 - When a man's ways please the LORD, he maketh even his enemies to be at peace with him.

ISAIAH 26:3 - Thou wilt keep him in perfect peace, whose mind is stayed on thee: because he trusteth in thee.

ISAIAH 32:17 - And the work of righteousness shall be peace; and the effect of righteousness quietness and assurance for ever.

ISAIAH 48:18 - O that thou hadst hearkened to my commandments! then had thy peace been as a river, and thy righteousness as the waves of the sea:

ISAIAH 53:5 - But he was wounded for our transgressions, he was bruised for our iniquities: the chastisement of our peace was upon him; and with his stripes we are healed.

JOHN 14:27 - Peace I leave with you, my peace I give unto you: not as the world giveth, give I unto you. Let not your heart be troubled, neither let it be afraid.

JOHN 16:33 - These things I have spoken unto you, that in me ye might have peace. In the world ye shall have tribulation: but be of good cheer; I have overcome the world.

ROMANS 5:1 - Therefore being justified by faith, we have peace with God through our Lord Jesus Christ:

ROMANS 8:6 - For to be carnally minded is death; but to be spiritually minded is life and peace.

ROMANS 14:17 - For the kingdom of God is not meat and drink; but righteousness, and peace, and joy in the Holy Ghost.

ROMANS 15:13 - Now the God of hope fill you with all joy and peace in believing, that ye may abound in hope, through the power of the Holy Ghost.

1 CORINTHIANS 1:3 - Grace be unto you, and peace, from God our Father, and from the Lord Jesus Christ.

GALATIANS 3:13 - Christ hath redeemed us from the curse of the law, being made a curse for us: for it is written, Cursed is every one that hangeth on a tree:

EPHESIANS 2:13-15 - But now in Christ Jesus ye who sometimes were far off are made nigh by the blood of Christ. For he is our peace, who hath made both one, and hath broken down the middle wall of partition between us; Having abolished in his flesh the enmity, even the law of commandments contained in ordinances; for to make in himself of twain one new man, so making peace;

PHILIPPIANS 2:5 - Let this mind be in you, which was also in Christ Jesus:

PHILIPPIANS 4:4-8 - Rejoice in the Lord alway: and again I say, Rejoice. Let your moderation be known unto all men. The Lord is at hand. Be careful for nothing; but in every thing by prayer and supplication with thanksgiving let your requests be made known unto God. And the peace of God, which passeth all understanding, shall keep your hearts and minds through Christ Jesus. Finally, brethren, whatsoever things are true, whatsoever things are honest, whatsoever things are just, whatsoever things are pure, whatsoever things are lovely, whatsoever things are of good report; if there be any virtue, and if there be any praise, think on these things.

COLOSSIANS 3:15 - And let the peace of God rule in your hearts, to the which also ye are called in one body; and be ye thankful.

2 THESSALONIANS 3:16 - Now the Lord of peace himself give you peace always by all means. The Lord be with you all.

2 TIMOTHY 1:7 - For God hath not given us the spirit of fear; but of power, and of love, and of a sound mind.

HEBREWS 12:3 - For consider him that endured such contradiction of sinners against himself, lest ye be wearied and faint in your minds.

1 PETER 5:6-7 - Humble yourselves therefore under the mighty hand of God, that he may exalt you in due time: Casting all your care upon him; for he careth for you.

PROSPERITY

GENESIS 12:1-2 - Now the Lord had said unto Abram, Get thee out of thy country, and from thy kindred, and from thy father's house, unto a land that I will shew thee: And I will make of thee a great nation, and I will bless thee, and make thy name great; and thou shalt be a blessing:

GALATIANS 3:29 - And if ye be Christ's, then are ye Abraham's seed, and heirs according to the promise.

GENESIS 24:40 - And he said unto me, The LORD, before whom I walk, will send his angel with thee, and prosper thy way;

DEUTERONOMY 8:18 - But thou shalt remember the LORD thy God: for it is he that giveth thee power to get wealth, that he may establish his covenant which he sware unto thy fathers, as it is this day.

DEUTERONOMY 15:7-8,10 - If there be among you a poor man of one of thy brethren within any of thy gates in thy land which the LORD thy God giveth thee, thou shalt not harden thine heart, nor shut thine hand from thy poor brother: But thou shalt open thine hand wide unto him, and shalt surely lend him sufficient for his need, in that which he wanteth. Thou shalt surely give him, and thine heart shall not be grieved when thou givest unto him: because that for this thing the LORD thy God shall bless thee in all thy works, and in all that thou puttest thine hand unto.

DEUTERONOMY 28:1-6,8,11-12 - And it shall come to pass, if thou shalt hearken diligently unto the voice of the LORD thy God, to observe and to do all his commandments which I command thee this day, that the LORD thy God will set thee on high above all nations of the earth: And all these blessings shall come on thee, and overtake thee, if thou shalt hearken unto the voice of the LORD thy God. Blessed shalt thou be in the city, and blessed shalt thou be in the field. Blessed shall be the fruit of thy body, and the fruit of thy ground, and the fruit of thy cattle, the increase of thy kine, and the flocks of thy sheep. Blessed shall be thy basket and thy store. Blessed shalt thou be when thou comest in, and blessed shalt thou be when thou goest out. The LORD shall command the blessing upon thee in thy storehouses, and in all that thou settest thine hand unto; and he shall bless thee in the land which the LORD thy God giveth thee. And the LORD shall make thee plenteous in goods, in the fruit of thy body, and in the fruit of thy cattle, and in the fruit of thy ground, in the land which the LORD sware unto thy fathers to give thee. The LORD shall open unto thee his good treasure, the heaven to give the rain unto thy land in his season, and to bless all the work of thine hand: and thou shalt lend unto many nations, and thou shalt not borrow.

DEUTERONOMY 29:9 - Keep therefore the words of this covenant, and do them, that ye may prosper in all that ye do.

JOSHUA 1:8 - This book of the law shall not depart out of thy mouth; but thou shalt meditate therein day and night, that thou mayest observe to do according to all that is written therein: for then thou shalt make thy way prosperous, and then thou shalt have good success.

2 CHRONICLES 26:5 - And he sought God in the days of Zechariah, who had understanding in the visions of God: and as long as he sought the LORD, God made him to prosper.

NEHEMIAH 2:20 - Then answered I them, and said unto them, The God of heaven, he will prosper us; therefore we his servants will arise and build: but ye have no portion, nor right, nor memorial, in Jerusalem.

JOB 22:25 - Yea, the Almighty shall be thy defence, and thou shalt have plenty of silver.

PSALMS 1:1-3 - Blessed is the man that walketh not in the counsel of the ungodly, nor standeth in the way of sinners, nor sitteth in the seat of the scornful. But his delight is in the law of the LORD; and in his law doth he meditate day and night. And he shall be like a tree planted by the rivers of water, that bringeth forth his fruit in his season; his leaf also shall not wither; and whatsoever he doeth shall prosper.

PSALMS 13:6 - I will sing unto the LORD, because he hath dealt bountifully with me.

PSALMS 23:1 - The LORD is my shepherd; I shall not want.

PSALMS 30:6 - And in my prosperity I said, I shall never be moved.

PSALMS 31:23 - O love the LORD, all ye his saints: for the LORD preserveth the faithful, and plentifully rewardeth the proud doer.

PSALMS 34:9-10 - O fear the LORD, ye his saints: for there is no want to them that fear him. The young lions do lack, and suffer hunger: but they that seek the LORD shall not want any good thing.

PSALMS 35:27 - Let them shout for joy, and be glad, that favour my righteous cause: yea, let them say continually, Let the LORD be magnified, which hath pleasure in the prosperity of his servant.

PSALMS 36:7-8 - How excellent is thy lovingkindness, O God! therefore the children of men put their trust under the shadow of thy wings. They shall be abundantly satisfied with the fatness of thy house; and thou shalt make them drink of the river of thy pleasures.

PSALMS 37:3 - Trust in the LORD, and do good; so shalt thou dwell in the land, and verily thou shalt be fed.

PSALMS 37:18-19 - The LORD knoweth the days of the upright: and their inheritance shall be for ever. They shall not be ashamed in the evil time: and in the days of famine they shall be satisfied.

PSALMS 66:12 - Thou hast caused men to ride over our heads; we went through fire and through water: but thou broughtest us out into a wealthy place.

PSALMS 68:19 - Blessed be the Lord, who daily loadeth us with benefits, even the God of our salvation. Selah.

PSALMS 84:11 - For the LORD God is a sun and shield: the LORD will give grace and glory: no good thing will he withhold from them that walk uprightly.

PSALMS 85:12 - Yea, the LORD shall give that which is good; and our land shall yield her increase.

PSALMS 92:12-14 - The righteous shall flourish like the palm tree: he shall grow like a cedar in Lebanon. Those that be planted in the house of the LORD shall flourish in the courts of our God. They shall still bring forth fruit in old age; they shall be fat and flourishing;

PSALMS 103:2,5 - Bless the LORD, O my soul, and forget not all his benefits: Who satisfieth thy mouth with good things; so that thy youth is renewed like the eagle's.

PSALMS 105:37 He brought them forth also with silver and gold: and there was not one feeble person among their tribes.

PSALMS 107:8-9 - Oh that men would praise the LORD for his goodness, and for his wonderful works to the children of men! For he satisfieth the longing soul, and filleth the hungry soul with goodness.

PSALMS 112:1-3 - Praise ye the LORD. Blessed is the man that feareth the LORD, that delighteth greatly in his commandments. His seed shall be mighty upon earth: the generation of the upright shall be blessed. Wealth and riches shall be in his house: and his righteousness endureth for ever.

PSALMS 115:14 - The LORD shall increase you more and more, you and your children.

PSALMS 118:25 - Save now, I beseech thee, O LORD: O LORD, I beseech thee, send now prosperity.

PSALMS 119:17 - Deal bountifully with thy servant, that I may live, and keep thy word.

PSALMS 119:65 - Thou hast dealt well with thy servant, O LORD, according unto thy word.

PSALMS 112:6-7 - Pray for the peace of Jerusalem: they shall prosper that love thee. Peace be within thy walls, and prosperity within thy palaces.

PROVERBS 3:9-10 - Honour the LORD with thy substance, and with the firstfruits of all thine increase: So shall thy barns be filled with plenty, and thy presses shall burst out with new wine.

PROVERBS 3:13,16 - Happy is the man that findeth wisdom, and the man that getteth understanding. Length of days is in her right hand; and in her left hand riches and honour.

PROVERBS 3.33 - The curse of the LORD is in the house of the wicked: but he blesseth the habitation of the just.

PROVERBS 8:12,18,20-21 - I wisdom dwell with prudence, and find out knowledge of witty inventions. Riches and honour are with me; yea, durable riches and righteousness. I lead in the way of righteousness, in the midst of the paths of judgment: That I may cause those that love me to inherit substance; and I will fill their treasures.

PROVERBS 10:4 - He becometh poor that dealeth with a slack hand: but the hand of the diligent maketh rich.

PROVERBS 10:22 - The blessing of the LORD, it maketh rich, and he addeth no sorrow with it.

PROVERBS 11:24-25 - There is that scattereth, and yet increaseth; and there is that withholdeth more than is meet, but it tendeth to poverty. The liberal soul shall be made fat: and he that watereth shall be watered also himself.

PROVERBS 11:28 - He that trusteth in his riches shall fall: but the righteous shall flourish as a branch.

PROVERBS 12:14 - A man shall be satisfied with good by the fruit of his mouth: and the recompense of a man's hands shall be rendered unto him.

PROVERBS 13:22 - A good man leaveth an inheritance to his children's children: and the wealth of the sinner is laid up for the just.

PROVERBS 14:11 - The house of the wicked shall be overthrown: but the tabernacle of the upright shall flourish.

PROVERBS 14:23 - In all labour there is profit: but the talk of the lips tendeth only to penury.

PROVERBS 16:20 - He that handleth a matter wisely shall find good: and whoso trusteth in the LORD, happy is he.

PROVERBS 19:23 - The fear of the LORD tendeth to life: and he that hath it shall abide satisfied; he shall not be visited with evil.

PROVERBS 22:4 - By humility and the fear of the LORD are riches, and honour, and life.

PROVERBS 28:10 - Whoso causeth the righteous to go astray in an evil way, he shall fall himself into his own pit: but the upright shall have good things in possession.

PROVERBS 28:20 - When the wicked rise, men hide themselves: but when they perish, the righteous increase.

PROVERBS 28:25 - He that is of a proud heart stirreth up strife: but he that putteth his trust in the LORD shall be made fat.

PROVERBS 28:27 - He that giveth unto the poor shall not lack: but he that hideth his eyes shall have many a curse.

ISAIAH 1:19 - If ye be willing and obedient, ye shall eat the good of the land:

JEREMIAH 17:7-8 - Blessed is the man that trusteth in the LORD, and whose hope the LORD is. For he shall be as a tree planted by the waters, and that spreadeth out her roots by the river, and shall not see when heat cometh, but her leaf shall be green; and shall not be careful in the year of drought, neither shall cease from yielding fruit.

MALACHI 3:10-11 - Bring ye all the tithes into the storehouse, that there may be meat in mine house, and prove me now herewith, saith the LORD of hosts, if I will not open you the windows of heaven, and pour you out a blessing, that there shall not be room enough to receive it. And I will rebuke the devourer for your sakes, and he shall not destroy the fruits of your ground; neither shall your vine cast her fruit before the time in the field, saith the LORD of hosts.

LUKE 6:38 - Give, and it shall be given unto you; good measure, pressed down, and shaken together, and running over, shall men give into your bosom. For with the same measure that ye mete withal it shall be measured to you again.

MATTHEW 6:31-33 - Therefore take no thought, saying, What shall we eat? or, What shall we drink? or, Wherewithal shall we be clothed? (For after all these things do the Gentiles seek:) for your heavenly Father knoweth that ye have need of all these things. But seek ye first the kingdom of God, and his righteousness; and all these things shall be added unto you.

MARK 10:29-30 - And Jesus answered and said, Verily I say unto you, There is no man that hath left house, or brethren, or sisters, or father, or mother, or wife, or children, or lands, for my sake, and the gospel's, But he shall receive an hundredfold now in this time, houses, and brethren, and sisters, and mothers, and children, and lands, with persecutions; and in the world to come eternal life.

JOHN 10:10 - The thief cometh not, but for to steal, and to kill, and to destroy: I am come that they might have life, and that they might have it more abundantly.

ROMANS 8:32 - He that spared not his own Son, but delivered him up for us all, how shall he not with him also freely give us all things?

ROMANS 10:12 - For there is no difference between the Jew and the Greek: for the same Lord over all is rich unto all that call upon him.

1 CORINTHIANS 2:9-10 - But as it is written, Eye hath not seen, nor ear heard, neither have entered into the heart of man, the things which God hath prepared for them that love him. But God hath revealed them unto us by his Spirit: for the Spirit searcheth all things, yea, the deep things of God.

2 CORINTHIANS 8:9 - For ye know the grace of our Lord Jesus Christ, that, though he was rich, yet for your sakes he became poor, that ye through his poverty might be rich.

2 CORINTHIANS 9:6-8 - But this I say, He which soweth sparingly shall reap also sparingly; and he which soweth bountifully shall reap also bountifully. Every man according as he purposeth in his heart, so let him give; not grudgingly, or of necessity: for God loveth a cheerful giver. And God is able to make all grace abound toward you; that ye, always having all sufficiency in all things, may abound to every good work:

GALATIANS 3:13-14 - Christ hath redeemed us from the curse of the law, being made a curse for us: for it is written, Cursed is every one that hangeth on a tree: That the blessing of Abraham might come on the Gentiles through Jesus Christ; that we might receive the promise of the Spirit through faith.

EPHESIANS 1:3 - Blessed be the God and Father of our Lord Jesus Christ, who hath blessed us with all spiritual blessings in heavenly places in Christ:

EPHESIANS 3:20 - Now unto him that is able to do exceeding abundantly above all that we ask or think, according to the power that worketh in us,

PHILIPPIANS 4:19 - But my God shall supply all your need according to his riches in glory by Christ Jesus.

1 THESSALONIANS 4:11-12 - And that ye study to be quiet, and to do your own business, and to work with your own hands, as we commanded you; That ye may walk honestly toward them that are without, and that ye may have lack of nothing.

1 TIMOTHY 6:17 - Charge them that are rich in this world, that they be not highminded, nor trust in uncertain riches, but in the living God, who giveth us richly all things to enjoy;

JAMES 1:4 - But let patience have her perfect work, that ye may be perfect and entire, wanting nothing.

1 PETER 3:10-11 - For he that will love life, and see good days, let him refrain his tongue from evil, and his lips that they speak no guile: Let him eschew evil, and do good; let him seek peace, and ensue it.

2 PETER 1:3 - According as his divine power hath given unto us all things that pertain unto life and godliness, through the knowledge of him that hath called us to glory and virtue:

3 JOHN 1:2 - Beloved, I wish above all things that thou mayest prosper and be in health, even as thy soul prospereth.

PROTECTION

DEUTERONOMY 31:6 - Be strong and of a good courage, fear not, nor be afraid of them: for the LORD thy God, he it is that doth go with thee; he will not fail thee, nor forsake thee.

LEVITICUS 25:18 - Wherefore ye shall do my statutes, and keep my judgments, and do them; and ye shall dwell in the land in safety.

JOB 22:25 - Yea, the Almighty shall be thy defence, and thou shalt have plenty of silver.

PSALMS 4:8 - I will both lay me down in peace, and sleep: for thou, LORD, only makest me dwell in safety.

PSALMS 7:10 - My defence is of God, which saveth the upright in heart.

PSALMS 17:4 - Concerning the works of men, by the word of thy lips I have kept me from the paths of the destroyer.

PSALMS 17:8 - Keep me as the apple of the eye, hide me under the shadow of thy wings,

PSALMS 20:1 - The LORD hear thee in the day of trouble; the name of the God of Jacob defend thee;

PSALMS 25:21 - Let integrity and uprightness preserve me; for I wait on thee.

PSALMS 31:23 - O love the LORD, all ye his saints: for the LORD preserveth the faithful, and plentifully rewardeth the proud doer.

PSALMS 32:6-7 - For this shall every one that is godly pray unto thee in a time when thou mayest be found: surely in the floods of great waters they shall not come nigh unto him. Thou art my hiding place; thou shalt preserve me from trouble; thou shalt compass me about with songs of deliverance. Selah.

PSALMS 33:17-20 - An horse is a vain thing for safety: neither shall he deliver any by his great strength. Behold, the eye of the LORD is upon them that fear him, upon them that hope in his mercy; To deliver their soul from death, and to keep them alive in famine. Our soul waiteth for the LORD: he is our help and our shield.

PSALMS 34:7 - The angel of the LORD encampeth round about them that fear him, and delivereth them.

PSALMS 36:6 - Thy righteousness is like the great mountains; thy judgments are a great deep: O LORD, thou preservest man and beast.

PSALMS 37:28 - For the LORD loveth judgment, and forsaketh not his saints; they are preserved for ever: but the seed of the wicked shall be cut off.

PSALMS 40:11 - Withhold not thou thy tender mercies from me, O LORD: let thy lovingkindness and thy truth continually preserve me.

PSALMS 41:1-2 - Blessed is he that considereth the poor: the LORD will deliver him in time of trouble. The LORD will preserve him, and keep him alive; and he shall be blessed upon the earth: and thou wilt not deliver him unto the will of his enemies.

PSALMS 46:1 - God is our refuge and strength, a very present help in trouble.

PSALMS 59:9 - Because of his strength will I wait upon thee: for God is my defence.

PSALMS 61:2-3 - From the end of the earth will I cry unto thee, when my heart is overwhelmed: lead me to the rock that is higher than I. For thou hast been a shelter for me, and a strong tower from the enemy.

PSALMS 91:1,4,7,10-12 - He that dwelleth in the secret place of the most High shall abide under the shadow of the Almighty. He shall cover thee with his feathers, and under his wings shalt thou trust: his truth shall be thy shield and buckler. A thousand shall fall at thy side, and ten thousand at thy right hand; but it shall not come nigh thee. There shall no evil befall thee, neither shall any plague come nigh thy dwelling. For he shall give his angels charge over thee, to keep thee in all thy ways. They shall bear thee up in their hands, lest thou dash thy foot against a stone.

PSALMS 97:10 - Ye that love the LORD, hate evil: he preserveth the souls of his saints; he delivereth them out of the hand of the wicked.

PSALMS 119:117 - Deal bountifully with thy servant, that I may live, and keep thy word.

PSALMS 121:7-8 - The LORD shall preserve thee from all evil: he shall preserve thy soul. The LORD shall preserve thy going out and thy coming in from this time forth, and even for evermore.

PSALMS 138:7 - Though I walk in the midst of trouble, thou wilt revive me: thou shalt stretch forth thine hand against the wrath of mine enemies, and thy right hand shall save me.

PSALMS 145:20 - The LORD preserveth all them that love him: but all the wicked will he destroy.

PROVERBS 1:20,33 - Wisdom crieth without; she uttereth her voice in the streets: But whoso hearkeneth unto me shall dwell safely, and shall be quiet from fear of evil.

PROVERBS 2:11 - Discretion shall preserve thee, understanding shall keep thee:

PROVERBS 3:21,23-26 - My son, let not them depart from thine eyes: keep sound wisdom and discretion: Then shalt thou walk in thy way safely, and thy foot shall not stumble. When thou liest down, thou shalt not be afraid: yea, thou shalt lie down, and thy sleep shall be sweet. Be not afraid of sudden fear, neither of the desolation of the wicked, when it cometh. For the LORD shall be thy confidence, and shall keep thy foot from being taken.

PROVERBS 4:5-6 - Get wisdom, get understanding: forget it not; neither decline from the words of my mouth. Forsake her not, and she shall preserve thee: love her, and she shall keep thee.

PROVERBS 11:14 - Where no counsel is, the people fall: but in the multitude of counsellors there is safety.

PROVERBS 12:21 - There shall no evil happen to the just: but the wicked shall be filled with mischief.

PROVERBS 14:3 - In the mouth of the foolish is a rod of pride: but the lips of the wise shall preserve them.

PROVERBS 18:10 - The name of the LORD is a strong tower: the righteous runneth into it, and is safe.

PROVERBS 21:31 - The horse is prepared against the day of battle: but safety is of the LORD.

PROVERBS 29:25 - The fear of man bringeth a snare: but whoso putteth his trust in the LORD shall be safe.

PROVERBS 30:5 - Every word of God is pure: he is a shield unto them that put their trust in him.

ECCLESIASTES 7:12 - For wisdom is a defence, and money is a defence: but the excellency of knowledge is, that wisdom giveth life to them that have it.

ISAIAH 43:2 - When thou passest through the waters, I will be with thee; and through the rivers, they shall not overflow thee: when thou walkest through the fire, thou shalt not be burned; neither shall the flame kindle upon thee.

HEBREWS 13:5-6 - Let your conversation be without covetousness; and be content with such things as ye have: for he hath said, I will never leave thee, nor forsake thee. So that we may boldly say, The Lord is my helper, and I will not fear what man shall do unto me.

MATTHEW 28:19-20 - Go ye therefore, and teach all nations, baptizing them in the name of the Father, and of the Son, and of the Holy Ghost: Teaching them to observe all things whatsoever I have commanded you: and, lo, I am with you alway, even unto the end of the world. Amen.

REDEMPTION

2 SAMUEL 4:9 - And David answered Rechab and Baanah his brother, the sons of Rimmon the Beerothite, and said unto them, As the LORD liveth, who hath redeemed my soul out of all adversity,

1 KINGS 1:29 - And the king sware, and said, As the LORD liveth, that hath redeemed my soul out of all distress,

JOB 19:25 - For I know that my redeemer liveth, and that he shall stand at the latter day upon the earth:

JOB 33:24 - Then he is gracious unto him, and saith, Deliver him from going down to the pit: I have found a ransom.

PSALMS 19:14 - Let the words of my mouth, and the meditation of my heart, be acceptable in thy sight, O LORD, my strength, and my redeemer.

PSALMS 34:22 - The LORD redeemeth the soul of his servants: and none of them that trust in him shall be desolate.

PSALMS 49:7-9 - None of them can by any means redeem his brother, nor give to God a ransom for him: (For the redemption of their soul is precious, and it ceaseth for ever:) That he should still live for ever, and not see corruption.

PSALMS 49:15 - But God will redeem my soul from the power of the grave: for he shall receive me. Selah.

PSALMS 71:23 - My lips shall greatly rejoice when I sing unto thee; and my soul, which thou hast redeemed.

PSALMS 78:35 - And they remembered that God was their rock, and the high God their redeemer.

PSALMS 103:2,4 - Bless the LORD, O my soul, and forget not all his benefits: Who redeemeth thy life from destruction; who crowneth thee with lovingkindness and tender mercies;

PSALMS 106:10 - And he saved them from the hand of him that hated them, and redeemed them from the hand of the enemy.

PSALMS 107:2 - Let the redeemed of the LORD say so, whom he hath redeemed from the hand of the enemy;

PSALMS 130:7 - Let Israel hope in the LORD: for with the LORD there is mercy, and with him is plenteous redemption.

ISAIAH 43:1 - But now thus saith the LORD that created thee, O Jacob, and he that formed thee, O Israel, Fear not: for I have redeemed thee, I have called thee by thy name; thou art mine.

ISAIAH 50:2 - Wherefore, when I came, was there no man? when I called, was there none to answer? Is my hand shortened at all, that it cannot redeem? or have I no power to deliver? behold, at my rebuke I dry up the sea, I make the rivers a wilderness: their fish stinketh, because there is no water, and dieth for thirst.

JEREMIAH 15:19,21 - Therefore thus saith the LORD, If thou return, then will I bring thee again, and thou shalt stand before me: and if thou take forth the precious from the vile, thou shalt be as my mouth: let them return unto thee; but return not thou unto them. And I will deliver thee out of the hand of the wicked, and I will redeem thee out of the hand of the terrible.

LAMENTATIONS 3:58 - O Lord, thou hast pleaded the causes of my soul; thou hast redeemed my life.

MATTHEW 20:28 - Even as the Son of man came not to be ministered unto, but to minister, and to give his life a ransom for many.

LUKE 21:28 - And when these things begin to come to pass, then look up, and lift up your heads; for your redemption draweth nigh.

ROMANS 3:24 - Being justified freely by his grace through the redemption that is in Christ Jesus:

ROMANS 8:2 - For the law of the Spirit of life in Christ Jesus hath made me free from the law of sin and death.

1 CORINTHIANS 1:30 - But of him are ye in Christ Jesus, who of God is made unto us wisdom, and righteousness, and sanctification, and redemption:

GALATIANS 3:13-14 - Christ hath redeemed us from the curse of the law, being made a curse for us: for it is written, Cursed is every one that hangeth on a tree: That the blessing of Abraham might come on the Gentiles through Jesus Christ; that we might receive the promise of the Spirit through faith.

GALATIANS 4:4-5 - But when the fulness of the time was come, God sent forth his Son, made of a woman, made under the law, To redeem them that were under the law, that we might receive the adoption of sons.

EPHESIANS 1:3-7 - Blessed be the God and Father of our Lord Jesus Christ, who hath blessed us with all spiritual blessings in heavenly places in Christ: According as he hath chosen us in him before the foundation of the world, that we should be holy and without blame before him in love: Having predestinated us unto the adoption of children by Jesus Christ to himself, according to the good pleasure of his will, To the praise of the glory of his grace, wherein he hath made us accepted in the beloved. In whom we have redemption through his blood, the forgiveness of sins, according to the riches of his grace;

COLOSSIANS 1:12-14 - Giving thanks unto the Father, which hath made us meet to be partakers of the inheritance of the saints in light: Who hath delivered us from the power of darkness, and hath translated us into the kingdom of his dear Son: In whom we have redemption through his blood, even the forgiveness of sins:

1 TIMOTHY 2:5-6 - For there is one God, and one mediator between God and men, the man Christ Jesus; Who gave himself a ransom for all, to be testified in due time.

TITUS 2:13-14 - Looking for that blessed hope, and the glorious appearing of the great God and our Saviour Jesus Christ; Who gave himself for us, that he might redeem us from all iniquity, and purify unto himself a peculiar people, zealous of good works.

HEBREWS 9:11-12,15 - But Christ being come an high priest of good things to come, by a greater and more perfect tabernacle, not made with hands, that is to say, not of this building; Neither by the blood of goats and calves, but by his own blood he entered in once into the holy place, having obtained eternal redemption for us. And for this cause he is the mediator of the new testament, that by means of death, for the redemption of the transgressions that were under the first testament, they which are called might receive the promise of eternal inheritance.

1 PETER 1:18-19 - Forasmuch as ye know that ye were not redeemed with corruptible things, as silver and gold, from your vain conversation received by tradition from your fathers; But with the precious blood of Christ, as of a lamb without blemish and without spot:

REVELATIONS 5:9-10 - And they sung a new song, saying, Thou art worthy to take the book, and to open the seals thereof: for thou wast slain, and hast redeemed us to God by thy blood out of every kindred, and tongue, and people, and nation; And hast made us unto our God kings and priests: and we shall reign on the earth.

RIGHTEOUSNESS

GENESIS 15:6 - And he believed in the LORD; and he counted it to him for righteousness.

GENESIS 18:26 - And the LORD said, If I find in Sodom fifty righteous within the city, then I will spare all the place for their sakes.

JOB 36:7 - He withdraweth not his eyes from the righteous: but with kings are they on the throne; yea, he doth establish them for ever, and they are exalted.

PSALMS 5:8 - Lead me, O LORD, in thy righteousness because of mine enemies; make thy way straight before my face.

PSALMS 5:12 - For thou, LORD, wilt bless the righteous; with favour wilt thou compass him as with a shield.

PSALMS 11:5 - The LORD trieth the righteous: but the wicked and him that loveth violence his soul hateth.

PSALMS 11:7 - For the righteous LORD loveth righteousness; his countenance doth behold the upright.

PSALMS 33:1 - Rejoice in the LORD, O ye righteous: for praise is comely for the upright.

PSALMS 34:15 - The eyes of the LORD are upon the righteous, and his ears are open unto their cry.

PSALMS 34:19 - Many are the afflictions of the righteous: but the LORD delivereth him out of them all.

PSALMS 37:17 - For the arms of the wicked shall be broken: but the LORD upholdeth the righteous.

PSALMS 37:25 - I have been young, and now am old; yet have I not seen the righteous forsaken, nor his seed begging bread.

PSALMS 37:30 - The mouth of the righteous speaketh wisdom, and his tongue talketh of judgment.

PSALMS 37:39 - But the salvation of the righteous is of the LORD: he is their strength in the time of trouble.

PSALMS 48:10 - According to thy name, O God, so is thy praise unto the ends of the earth: thy right hand is full of righteousness.

PSALMS 55:22 - Cast thy burden upon the LORD, and he shall sustain thee: he shall never suffer the righteous to be moved.

PSALMS 65:5 - By terrible things in righteousness wilt thou answer us, O God of our salvation; who art the confidence of all the ends of the earth, and of them that are afar off upon the sea:

PSALMS 71:1-2 - In thee, O LORD, do I put my trust: let me never be put to confusion. Deliver me in thy righteousness, and cause me to escape: incline thine ear unto me, and save me.

PSALMS 71:15-16 - My mouth shall show forth thy righteousness and thy salvation all the day; for I know not the numbers thereof. I will go in the strength of the Lord GOD: I will make mention of thy righteousness, even of thine only.

PSALMS 85:10 - Mercy and truth are met together; righteousness and peace have kissed each other.

PSALMS 89:16 - In thy name shall they rejoice all the day: and in thy righteousness shall they be exalted.

PSALMS 92:12 - The righteous shall flourish like the palm tree: he shall grow like a cedar in Lebanon.

PSALMS 103:17-18 - But the mercy of the LORD is from everlasting to everlasting upon them that fear him, and his righteousness unto children's children; To such as keep his covenant, and to those that remember his commandments to do them.

PSALMS 106:30-31 - Then stood up Phinehas, and executed judgment: and so the plague was stayed. And that was counted unto him for righteousness unto all generations for evermore.

PSALMS 111:3 - His work is honourable and glorious: and his righteousness endureth for ever.

PSALMS 112:4,9 - Unto the upright there ariseth light in the darkness: he is gracious, and full of compassion, and righteous. He hath dispersed, he hath given to the poor; his righteousness endureth for ever; his horn shall be exalted with honour.

PSALMS 119:172 - My tongue shall speak of thy word: for all thy commandments are righteousness.

PSALMS 146:8 - The LORD openeth the eyes of the blind: the LORD raiseth them that are bowed down: the LORD loveth the righteous:

PROVERBS 2:7 - He layeth up sound wisdom for the righteous: he is a buckler to them that walk uprightly.

PROVERBS 3:32 - For the froward is abomination to the LORD: but his secret is with the righteous.

PROVERBS 8:8 - All the words of my mouth are in righteousness; there is nothing froward or perverse in them.

PROVERBS 10:2-3 - Treasures of wickedness profit nothing: but righteousness delivereth from death. The LORD will not suffer the soul of the righteous to famish: but he casteth away the substance of the wicked.

PROVERBS 10:6-7 - Blessings are upon the head of the just: but violence covereth the mouth of the wicked. The memory of the just is blessed: but the name of the wicked shall rot.

PROVERBS 10:16 - The labour of the righteous tendeth to life: the fruit of the wicked to sin.

PROVERBS 10:21 - The lips of the righteous feed many: but fools die for want of wisdom.

PROVERBS 10:24 - The fear of the wicked, it shall come upon him: but the desire of the righteous shall be granted.

PROVERBS 10:30 - The righteous shall never be removed: but the wicked shall not inhabit the earth.

PROVERBS 10:32 - The lips of the righteous know what is acceptable: but the mouth of the wicked speaketh frowardness.

PROVERBS 11:3 - The integrity of the upright shall guide them: but the perverseness of transgressors shall destroy them.

PROVERBS 11:5 - The righteousness of the perfect shall direct his way: but the wicked shall fall by his own wickedness.

PROVERBS 11:6 - The righteousness of the upright shall deliver them: but transgressors shall be taken in their own naughtiness.

PROVERBS 11:21 - Though hand join in hand, the wicked shall not be unpunished: but the seed of the righteous shall be delivered.

PROVERBS 11:30 - The fruit of the righteous is a tree of life; and he that winneth souls is wise.

PROVERBS 12:3 - A man shall not be established by wickedness: but the root of the righteous shall not be moved.

PROVERBS 12:7 - The wicked are overthrown, and are not: but the house of the righteous shall stand.

PROVERBS 12:12 - The wicked desireth the net of evil men: but the root of the righteous yieldeth fruit.

PROVERBS 12:17 - He that speaketh truth showeth forth righteousness: but a false witness deceit.

PROVERBS 12:28 - In the way of righteousness is life; and in the pathway thereof there is no death.

PROVERBS 13:6 - Righteousness keepeth him that is upright in the way: but wickedness overthroweth the sinner.

PROVERBS 13:9 - The light of the righteous rejoiceth: but the lamp of the wicked shall be put out.

PROVERBS 13:21 - Evil pursueth sinners: but to the righteous good shall be repayed.

PROVERBS 13:25 - The righteous eateth to the satisfying of his soul: but the belly of the wicked shall want.

PROVERBS 14:9 - Fools make a mock at sin: but among the righteous there is favour.

PROVERBS 14:32 - The wicked is driven away in his wickedness: but the righteous hath hope in his death.

PROVERBS 14:34 - Righteousness exalteth a nation: but sin is a reproach to any people.

PROVERBS 15:6 - In the house of the righteous is much treasure: but in the revenues of the wicked is trouble.

PROVERBS 15:19 - The way of the slothful man is as an hedge of thorns: but the way of the righteous is made plain.

PROVERBS 15:29 - The LORD is far from the wicked: but he heareth the prayer of the righteous.

PROVERBS 20:7 - The just man walketh in his integrity: his children are blessed after him.

PROVERBS 21:21 - He that followeth after righteousness and mercy findeth life, righteousness, and honour.

PROVERBS 24:16 - For a just man falleth seven times, and riseth up again: but the wicked shall fall into mischief.

PROVERBS 28:1 - The wicked flee when no man pursueth: but the righteous are bold as a lion.

PROVERBS 28:10 - Whoso causeth the righteous to go astray in an evil way, he shall fall himself into his own pit: but the upright shall have good things in possession.

PROVERBS 28:18 - Whoso walketh uprightly shall be saved: but he that is perverse in his ways shall fall at once.

PROVERBS 29:7 - The righteous considereth the cause of the poor: but the wicked regardeth not to know it.

ISAIAH 32:17 - And the work of righteousness shall be peace; and the effect of righteousness quietness and assurance for ever.

ISAIAH 51:5-6 - My righteousness is near; my salvation is gone forth, and mine arms shall judge the people; the isles shall wait upon me, and on mine arm shall they trust. Lift up your eyes to the heavens, and look upon the earth beneath: for the heavens shall vanish away like smoke, and the earth shall wax old like a garment, and they that dwell therein shall die in like manner: but my salvation shall be for ever, and my righteousness shall not be abolished.

ISAIAH 54:14,17 - In righteousness shalt thou be established: thou shalt be far from oppression; for thou shalt not fear: and from terror; for it shall not come near thee. No weapon that is formed against thee shall prosper; and every tongue that shall rise against thee in judgment thou shalt condemn. This is the heritage of the servants of the LORD, and their righteousness is of me, saith the LORD.

JEREMIAH 9:24 - But let him that glorieth glory in this, that he understandeth and knoweth me, that I am the LORD which exercise lovingkindness, judgment, and righteousness, in the earth: for in these things I delight, saith the LORD.

JEREMIAH 23:6 - In his days Judah shall be saved, and Israel shall dwell safely: and this is his name whereby he shall be called, THE LORD OUR RIGHTEOUS-NESS.

HABAKKUK 2:4 - Behold, his soul which is lifted up is not upright in him: but the just shall live by his faith.

MATTHEW 5:6 - Blessed are they which do hunger and thirst after righteousness: for they shall be filled.

MATTHEW 5:10 - Blessed are they which are persecuted for righteousness' sake: for theirs is the kingdom of heaven.

MATTHEW 6:33 - But seek ye first the kingdom of God, and his righteousness; and all these things shall be added unto you.

MATTHEW 25:46 - And these shall go away into everlasting punishment: but the righteous into life eternal.

ACTS 13:39 - And by him all that believe are justified from all things, from which ye could not be justified by the law of Moses.

ROMANS 1:16-17 - For I am not ashamed of the gospel of Christ: for it is the power of God unto salvation to every one that believeth; to the Jew first, and also to the Greek. For therein is the righteousness of God revealed from faith to faith: as it is written, The just shall live by faith.

ROMANS 2:13 - For not the hearers of the law are just before God, but the doers of the law shall be justified.

ROMANS 3:21-22 - But now the righteousness of God without the law is manifested, being witnessed by the law and the prophets; Even the righteousness of God which is by faith of Jesus Christ unto all and upon all them that believe: for there is no difference:

ROMANS 4:3 - For what saith the scripture? Abraham believed God, and it was counted unto him for righteousness.

ROMANS 4:11 - And he received the sign of circumcision, a seal of the righteousness of the faith which he had yet being uncircumcised: that he might be the father of all them that believe, though they be not circumcised; that righteousness might be imputed unto them also:

ROMANS 5:1 - Therefore being justified by faith, we have peace with God through our Lord Jesus Christ:

ROMANS 5:17 - For if by one man's offence death reigned by one; much more they which receive abundance of grace and of the gift of righteousness shall reign in life by one, Jesus Christ.

ROMANS 10:4 - For Christ is the end of the law for righteousness to every one that believeth.

ROMANS 10:10 - For with the heart man believeth unto righteousness; and with the mouth confession is made unto salvation.

ROMANS 14:17 - For the kingdom of God is not meat and drink; but righteousness, and peace, and joy in the Holy Ghost.

1 CORINTHIANS 1:30 - But of him are ye in Christ Jesus, who of God is made unto us wisdom, and righteousness, and sanctification, and redemption:

1 CORINTHIANS 15:34 - Awake to righteousness, and sin not; for some have not the knowledge of God: I speak this to your shame.

2 CORINTHIANS 5:21 - For he hath made him to be sin for us, who knew no sin; that we might be made the righteousness of God in him.

GALATIANS 2:16 - Knowing that a man is not justified by the works of the law, but by the faith of Jesus Christ, even we have believed in Jesus Christ, that we might be justified by the faith of Christ, and not by the works of the law: for by the works of the law shall no flesh be justified.

GALATIANS 3:24 - Wherefore the law was our schoolmaster to bring us unto Christ, that we might be justified by faith.

EPHESIANS 4:24 -.And that ye put on the new man, which after God is created in righteousness and true holiness.

PHILIPPIANS 3:9 - And be found in him, not having mine own righteousness, which is of the law, but that which is through the faith of Christ, the righteousness which is of God by faith:

1 TIMOTHY 6:11 - But thou, O man of God, flee these things; and follow after righteousness, godliness, faith, love, patience, meekness.

HEBREWS 12:11 - Now no chastening for the present seemeth to be joyous, but grievous: nevertheless afterward it yieldeth the peaceable fruit of righteousness unto them which are exercised thereby.

JAMES 1:20 - For the wrath of man worketh not the righteousness of God.

JAMES 5:16 - Confess your faults one to another, and pray one for another, that ye may be healed. The effectual fervent prayer of a righteous man availeth much.

TITUS 2:11-12 - For the grace of God that bringeth salvation hath appeared to all men, Teaching us that, denying ungodliness and worldly lusts, we should live soberly, righteously, and godly, in this present world;

TITUS 3:7 - That being justified by his grace, we should be made heirs according to the hope of eternal life.

1 PETER 2:24 - Who his own self bare our sins in his own body on the tree, that we, being dead to sins, should live unto righteousness: by whose stripes ye were healed.

1 PETER 3:12 - For the eyes of the Lord are over the righteous, and his ears are open unto their prayers: but the face of the Lord is against them that do evil.

1 JOHN 2:29 - If ye know that he is righteous, ye know that every one that doeth righteousness is born of him.

1 JOHN 3:7 - Little children, let no man deceive you: he that doeth righteousness is righteous, even as he is righteous.

REVELATION 22:11 - He that is unjust, let him be unjust still: and he which is filthy, let him be filthy still: and he that is righteous, let him be righteous still: and he that is holy, let him be holy still.

SCRIPTURES TO LIVE BY

SALVATION
(ETERNAL LIFE)

PSALMS 27:1 - The LORD is my light and my salvation; whom shall I fear? the LORD is the strength of my life; of whom shall I be afraid?

PSALMS 62:1 - Truly my soul waiteth upon God: from him cometh my salvation.

PSALMS 68:20 - He that is our God is the God of salvation; and unto GOD the Lord belong the issues from death.

PSALMS 98:2 - The LORD hath made known his salvation: his righteousness hath he openly showed in the sight of the heathen.

PSALMS 118:14 - The LORD is my strength and song, and is become my salvation.

PSALMS 119:41 - Let thy mercies come also unto me, O LORD, even thy salvation, according to thy word.

PSALMS 149:4 - For the LORD taketh pleasure in his people: he will beautify the meek with salvation.

PROVERBS 12:28 - In the way of righteousness is life; and in the pathway thereof there is no death.

JOHN 1:12 - But as many as received him, to them gave he power to become the sons of God, even to them that believe on his name:

JOHN 3:3 - Jesus answered and said unto him, Verily, verily, I say unto thee, Except a man be born again, he cannot see the kingdom of God.

JOHN 3:16 - For God so loved the world, that he gave his only begotten Son, that whosoever believeth in him should not perish, but have everlasting life.

JOHN 3:36 - He that believeth on the Son hath everlasting life: and he that believeth not the Son shall not see life; but the wrath of God abideth on him.

JOHN 5:24 - Verily, verily, I say unto you, He that heareth my word, and believeth on him that sent me, hath everlasting life, and shall not come into condemnation; but is passed from death unto life.

JOHN 6:40 - And this is the will of him that sent me, that every one which seeth the Son, and believeth on him, may have everlasting life: and I will raise him up at the last day.

JOHN 6:47 - Verily, verily, I say unto you, He that believeth on me hath everlasting life.

JOHN 10:27-28 - My sheep hear my voice, and I know them, and they follow me: And I give unto them eternal life; and they shall never perish, neither shall any man pluck them out of my hand.

ACTS 2:38 - Then Peter said unto them, Repent, and be baptized every one of you in the name of Jesus Christ for the remission of sins, and ye shall receive the gift of the Holy Ghost.

ACTS 4:10,12 - Be it known unto you all, and to all the people of Israel, that by the name of Jesus Christ of Nazareth, whom ye crucified, whom God raised from the dead, even by him doth this man stand here before you whole. Neither is there salvation in any other: for there is none other name under heaven given among men, whereby we must be saved.

ACTS 16:30-31 - And brought them out, and said, Sirs, what must I do to be saved? And they said, Believe on the Lord Jesus Christ, and thou shalt be saved, and thy house.

ROMANS 3:23, 6:23 - For all have sinned, and come short of the glory of God; For the wages of sin is death; but the gift of God is eternal life through Jesus Christ our Lord.

ROMANS 10:9-10 - That if thou shalt confess with thy mouth the Lord Jesus, and shalt believe in thine heart that God hath raised him from the dead, thou shalt be saved. For with the heart man believeth unto righteousness; and with the mouth confession is made unto salvation.

ROMANS 10:13 - For whosoever shall call upon the name of the Lord shall be saved.

2 CORINTHIANS 5:17 - Therefore if any man be in Christ, he is a new creature: old things are passed away; behold, all things are become new.

EPHESIANS 2:8-9 - For by grace are ye saved through faith; and that not of yourselves: it is the gift of God: Not of works, lest any man should boast.

1 TIMOTHY 2:3-4 - For this is good and acceptable in the sight of God our Saviour; Who will have all men to be saved, and to come unto the knowledge of the truth.

2 TIMOTHY 1:9 - Who hath saved us, and called us with an holy calling, not according to our works, but according to his own purpose and grace, which was given us in Christ Jesus before the world began,

TITUS 3:5 - Not by works of righteousness which we have done, but according to his mercy he saved us, by the washing of regeneration, and renewing of the Holy Ghost;

1 PETER 1:23 - Being born again, not of corruptible seed, but of incorruptible, by the word of God, which liveth and abideth for ever.

2 PETER 3:9 - The Lord is not slack concerning his promise, as some men count slackness; but is longsuffering to us-ward, not willing that any should perish, but that all should come to repentance.

1 JOHN 2:24-25 - Let that therefore abide in you, which ye have heard from the beginning. If that which ye have heard from the beginning shall remain in you, ye also shall continue in the Son, and in the Father. And this is the promise that he hath promised us, even eternal life.

1 JOHN 5:11-12 - And this is the record, that God hath given to us eternal life, and this life is in his Son. He that hath the Son hath life; and he that hath not the Son of God hath not life.

1 JOHN 5:13 - These things have I written unto you that believe on the name of the Son of God; that ye may know that ye have eternal life, and that ye may believe on the name of the Son of God.

SLEEP
(AND REST)

EXODUS 23:12 - Six days thou shalt do thy work, and on the seventh day thou shalt rest: that thine ox and thine ass may rest, and the son of thy handmaid, and the stranger, may be refreshed.

EXODUS 33:14 - And he said, My presence shall go with thee, and I will give thee rest.

RUTH 3:1 - Then Naomi her mother in law said unto her, My daughter, shall I not seek rest for thee, that it may be well with thee?

1 KINGS 5:4 - But now the LORD my God hath given me rest on every side, so that there is neither adversary nor evil occurrent.

1 KINGS 8:56 - Blessed be the LORD, that hath given rest unto his people Israel, according to all that he promised: there hath not failed one word of all his good promise, which he promised by the hand of Moses his servant.

JOB 11:18-19 - And thou shalt be secure, because there is hope; yea, thou shalt dig about thee, and thou shalt take thy rest in safety. Also thou shalt lie down, and none shall make thee afraid; yea, many shall make suit unto thee.

PSALMS 3:5 - I laid me down and slept; I awaked; for the LORD sustained me.

PSALMS 4:8 - I will both lay me down in peace, and sleep: for thou, LORD, only makest me dwell in safety.

PSALMS 16:8-9 - I have set the LORD always before me: because he is at my right hand, I shall not be moved. Therefore my heart is glad, and my glory rejoiceth: my flesh also shall rest in hope.

PSALMS 37:7 - Rest in the LORD, and wait patiently for him: fret not thyself because of him who prospereth in his way, because of the man who bringeth wicked devices to pass.

PSALMS 94:12-13 - Blessed is the man whom thou chastenest, O LORD, and teachest him out of thy law; That thou mayest give him rest from the days of adversity, until the pit be digged for the wicked.

PSALMS 116:7 - Return unto thy rest, O my soul; for the LORD hath dealt bountifully with thee.

PSALMS 121:2-3 - My help cometh from the LORD, which made heaven and earth. He will not suffer thy foot to be moved: he that keepeth thee will not slumber.

PSALMS 127:2 - It is vain for you to rise up early, to sit up late, to eat the bread of sorrows: for so he giveth his beloved sleep.

PROVERBS 3:24 - When thou liest down, thou shalt not be afraid: yea, thou shalt lie down, and thy sleep shall be sweet.

PROVERBS 6:20-22 - My son, keep thy father's commandment, and forsake not the law of thy mother: Bind them continually upon thine heart, and tie them about thy neck. When thou goest, it shall lead thee; when thou sleepest, it shall keep thee; and when thou awakest, it shall talk with thee.

PROVERBS 29:17 - Correct thy son, and he shall give thee rest; yea, he shall give delight unto thy soul.

ECCLESIASTES 5:12 - The sleep of a labouring man is sweet, whether he eat little or much: but the abundance of the rich will not suffer him to sleep.

ISAIAH 28:11-12 - For with stammering lips and another tongue will he speak to this people. To whom he said, This is the rest wherewith ye may cause the weary to rest; and this is the refreshing: yet they would not hear.

JEREMIAH 6:16 - Thus saith the LORD, Stand ye in the ways, and see, and ask for the old paths, where is the good way, and walk therein, and ye shall find rest for your souls. But they said, We will not walk therein.

JEREMIAH 31:25-26 - For I have satiated the weary soul, and I have replenished every sorrowful soul. Upon this I awaked, and beheld; and my sleep was sweet unto me.

MATTHEW 8:24 - And, behold, there arose a great tempest in the sea, insomuch that the ship was covered with the waves: but he was asleep.

MATTHEW 11:28-29 - Come unto me, all ye that labour and are heavy laden, and I will give you rest. Take my yoke upon you, and learn of me; for I am meek and lowly in heart: and ye shall find rest unto your souls.

MARK 6:31 - And he said unto them, Come ye your-selves apart into a desert place, and rest a while: for there were many coming and going, and they had no leisure so much as to eat.

ACTS 2:26 - Therefore did my heart rejoice, and my tongue was glad; moreover also my flesh shall rest in hope:

2 THESSALONIANS 1:7 - And to you who are trou-bled rest with us, when the Lord Jesus shall be revealed from heaven with his mighty angels,

HEBREWS 4:9 - There remaineth therefore a rest to the people of God.

STRENGTH

EXODUS 15:2 - The LORD is my strength and song, and he is become my salvation: he is my God, and I will prepare him an habitation; my father's God, and I will exalt him.

EXODUS 15:13 - Thou in thy mercy hast led forth the people which thou hast redeemed: thou hast guided them in thy strength unto thy holy habitation.

DEUTERONOMY 11:8 - Therefore shall ye keep all the commandments which I command you this day, that ye may be strong, and go in and possess the land, whither ye go to possess it;

JOSHUA 1:7 - Only be thou strong and very courageous, that thou mayest observe to do according to all the law, which Moses my servant commanded thee: turn not from it to the right hand or to the left, that thou mayest prosper whithersoever thou goest.

2 SAMUEL 22:33 - God is my strength and power: And he maketh my way perfect.

1 CHRONICLES 16:11 - Seek the LORD and his strength, seek his face continually.

NEHEMIAH 8:10 - Then he said unto them, Go your way, eat the fat, and drink the sweet, and send portions unto them for whom nothing is prepared: for this day is holy unto our Lord: neither be ye sorry; for the joy of the LORD is your strength.

JOB 12:13 - With him is wisdom and strength, he hath counsel and understanding.

PSALMS 18:2 - The LORD is my rock, and my fortress, and my deliverer; my God, my strength, in whom I will trust; my buckler, and the horn of my salvation, and my high tower.

PSALMS 18:39 - For thou hast girded me with strength unto the battle: thou hast subdued under me those that rose up against me.

PSALMS 19:14 - Let the words of my mouth, and the meditation of my heart, be acceptable in thy sight, O LORD, my strength, and my redeemer.

PSALMS 24:8 - Who is this King of glory? The LORD strong and mighty, the LORD mighty in battle.

PSALMS 27:1 - The LORD is my light and my salvation; whom shall I fear? the LORD is the strength of my life; of whom shall I be afraid?

PSALMS 27:14 - Wait on the LORD: be of good courage, and he shall strengthen thine heart: wait, I say, on the LORD.

PSALMS 28:7-8 - The LORD is my strength and my shield; my heart trusted in him, and I am helped: therefore my heart greatly rejoiceth; and with my song will I praise him. The LORD is their strength, and he is the saving strength of his anointed.

PSALMS 29:11 - The LORD will give strength unto his people; the LORD will bless his people with peace.

PSALMS 31:4 - Pull me out of the net that they have laid privily for me: for thou art my strength.

PSALMS 31:24 - Be of good courage, and he shall strengthen your heart, all ye that hope in the LORD.

PSALMS 37:39 - But the salvation of the righteous is of the LORD: he is their strength in the time of trouble.

PSALMS 41:3 - The LORD will strengthen him upon the bed of languishing: thou wilt make all his bed in his sickness.

PSALMS 46:1 - God is our refuge and strength, a very present help in trouble.

PSALMS 68:35 - O God, thou art terrible out of thy holy places: the God of Israel is he that giveth strength and power unto his people. Blessed be God.

PSALMS 73:26 - My flesh and my heart faileth: but God is the strength of my heart, and my portion for ever.

PSALMS 81:1 - Sing aloud unto God our strength: make a joyful noise unto the God of Jacob.

PSALMS 84:5 - Blessed is the man whose strength is in thee; in whose heart are the ways of them.

PSALMS 103:2,5 - Bless the LORD, O my soul, and forget not all his benefits: Who satisfieth thy mouth with good things; so that thy youth is renewed like the eagle's.

PSALMS 105:24 - And he increased his people greatly; and made them stronger than their enemies.

PSALMS 118:14 - The LORD is my strength and song, and is become my salvation.

PSALMS 119:28 - My soul melteth for heaviness: strengthen thou me according unto thy word.

PSALMS 138:3 - In the day when I cried thou answeredst me, and strengthenedst me with strength in my soul.

PROVERBS 8:14 - Counsel is mine, and sound wisdom: I am understanding; I have strength.

PROVERBS 11:16 - A gracious woman retaineth honour: and strong men retain riches.

PROVERBS 18:10 - The name of the LORD is a strong tower: the righteous runneth into it, and is safe.

PROVERBS 24:5 - A wise man is strong; yea, a man of knowledge increaseth strength.

PROVERBS 24:10 - If thou faint in the day of adversity, thy strength is small.

ECCLESIASTES 7:19 - Wisdom strengtheneth the wise more than ten mighty men which are in the city.

ISAIAH 30:15 - in quietness and in confidence shall be your strength:

ISAIAH 35:3-4 - Strengthen ye the weak hands, and confirm the feeble knees. Say to them that are of a fearful heart, Be strong, fear not: behold, your God will come with vengeance, even God with a recompense; he will come and save you.

ISAIAH 40:29,31 - He giveth power to the faint; and to them that have no might he increaseth strength. But they that wait upon the LORD shall renew their strength; they shall mount up with wings as eagles; they shall run, and not be weary; and they shall walk, and not faint.

ISAIAH 41:10 - Fear thou not; for I am with thee: be not dismayed; for I am thy God: I will strengthen thee; yea, I will help thee; yea, I will uphold thee with the right hand of my righteousness.

EZEKIEL 34:15-16 - I will feed my flock, and I will cause them to lie down, saith the Lord GOD. I will seek that which was lost, and bring again that which was driven away, and will bind up that which was broken, and will strengthen that which was sick: but I will destroy the fat and the strong; I will feed them with judgment.

DANIEL 11:32 - And such as do wickedly against the covenant shall he corrupt by flatteries: but the people that do know their God shall be strong, and do exploits.

JOEL 2:11 - And the LORD shall utter his voice before his army: for his camp is very great: for he is strong that executeth his word: for the day of the LORD is great and very terrible; and who can abide it?

JOEL 3:10 - Beat your plowshares into swords, and your pruninghooks into spears: let the weak say, I am strong.

MARK 12:30 - And thou shalt love the Lord thy God with all thy heart, and with all thy soul, and with all thy mind, and with all thy strength: this is the first commandment.

ACTS 3:16 - And his name through faith in his name hath made this man strong, whom ye see and know: yea, the faith which is by him hath given him this perfect soundness in the presence of you all.

ROMANS 4:20-21 - He staggered not at the promise of God through unbelief; but was strong in faith, giving glory to God; And being fully persuaded that, what he had promised, he was able also to perform.

ROMANS 15:1 - We then that are strong ought to bear the infirmities of the weak, and not to please ourselves.

1 CORINTHIANS 16:13 - Watch ye, stand fast in the faith, quit you like men, be strong.

2 CORINTHIANS 12:9-10 - And he said unto me, My grace is sufficient for thee: for my strength is made perfect in weakness. Most gladly therefore will I rather glory in my infirmities, that the power of Christ may rest upon me. Therefore I take pleasure in infirmities, in reproaches, in necessities, in persecutions, in distresses for Christ's sake: for when I am weak, then am I strong.

EPHESIANS 3:16 - That he would grant you, according to the riches of his glory, to be strengthened with might by his Spirit in the inner man;

EPHESIANS 6:10 - Finally, my brethren, be strong in the Lord, and in the power of his might.

PHILIPPIANS 4:13 - I can do all things through Christ which strengtheneth me.

COLOSSIANS 1:11 - Strengthened with all might, according to his glorious power, unto all patience and longsuffering with joyfulness;

2 TIMOTHY 2:1 - Thou therefore, my son, be strong in the grace that is in Christ Jesus.

HEBREWS 11:33-34 - Who through faith subdued kingdoms, wrought righteousness, obtained promises, stopped the mouths of lions, Quenched the violence of fire, escaped the edge of the sword, out of weakness were made strong, waxed valiant in fight, turned to flight the armies of the aliens.

1 PETER 5:10 - But the God of all grace, who hath called us unto his eternal glory by Christ Jesus, after that ye have suffered a while, make you perfect, stablish, strengthen, settle you.

1 JOHN 2:14 - I have written unto you, fathers, because ye have known him that is from the beginning. I have written unto you, young men, because ye are strong, and the word of God abideth in you, and ye have overcome the wicked one.

REVELATION 5:12 - Saying with a loud voice, Worthy is the Lamb that was slain to receive power, and riches, and wisdom, and strength, and honour, and glory, and blessing.

REVELATION 3:2 - Be watchful, and strengthen the things which remain, that are ready to die: for I have not found thy works perfect before God.

SUCCESS

GENESIS 24:40 - And he said unto me, The LORD, before whom I walk, will send his angel with thee, and prosper thy way; and thou shalt take a wife for my son of my kindred, and of my father's house:

GENESIS 39:3 - And his master saw that the LORD was with him, and that the LORD made all that he did to prosper in his hand.

GENESIS 39:22-23 - And the keeper of the prison committed to Joseph's hand all the prisoners that were in the prison; and whatsoever they did there, he was the doer of it. The keeper of the prison looked not to any thing that was under his hand; because the LORD was with him, and that which he did, the LORD made it to prosper.

DEUTERONOMY 29:9 - Keep therefore the words of this covenant, and do them, that ye may prosper in all that ye do.

DEUTERONOMY 31:6 - Be strong and of a good courage, fear not, nor be afraid of them: for the LORD thy God, he it is that doth go with thee; he will not fail thee, nor forsake thee.

JOSHUA 1:8 - This book of the law shall not depart out of thy mouth; but thou shalt meditate therein day and night, that thou mayest observe to do according to all that is written therein: for then thou shalt make thy way prosperous, and then thou shalt have good success.

JOSHUA 21:45 - There failed not ought of any good thing which the LORD had spoken unto the house of Israel; all came to pass.

1 KINGS 2:3 - And keep the charge of the LORD thy God, to walk in his ways, to keep his statutes, and his commandments, and his judgments, and his testimonies, as it is written in the law of Moses, that thou mayest prosper in all that thou doest, and whithersoever thou turnest thyself:

2 KINGS 18:7 - And the LORD was with him; and he prospered whithersoever he went forth: and he rebelled against the king of Assyria, and served him not.

2 CHRONICLES 20:20 - And they rose early in the morning, and went forth into the wilderness of Tekoa: and as they went forth, Jehoshaphat stood and said, Hear me, O Judah, and ye inhabitants of Jerusalem; Believe in the LORD your God, so shall ye be established; believe his prophets, so shall ye prosper.

JOB 36:11 - If they obey and serve him, they shall spend their days in prosperity, and their years in pleasures.

PSALMS 1:1-3 - Blessed is the man that walketh not in the counsel of the ungodly, nor standeth in the way of sinners, nor sitteth in the seat of the scornful. But his delight is in the law of the LORD; and in his law doth he meditate day and night. And he shall be like a tree planted by the rivers of water, that bringeth forth his fruit in his season; his leaf also shall not wither; and whatsoever he doeth shall prosper.

PSALMS 30:6 - And in my prosperity I said, I shall never be moved.

PSALMS 35:27 - Let them shout for joy, and be glad, that favour my righteous cause: yea, let them say continually, Let the LORD be magnified, which hath pleasure in the prosperity of his servant.

PSALMS 89:33 - Nevertheless my lovingkindness will I not utterly take from him, nor suffer my faithfulness to fail.

PSALMS 122:6 - Pray for the peace of Jerusalem: they shall prosper that love thee.

PROVERBS 4:7-8 - Wisdom is the principal thing; therefore get wisdom: and with all thy getting get understanding. Exalt her, and she shall promote thee: she shall bring thee to honour, when thou dost embrace her.

ZEPHANIAH 3:5 - The just LORD is in the midst thereof; he will not do iniquity: every morning doth he bring his judgment to light, he faileth not; but the unjust knoweth no shame.

LUKE 12:33 - Sell that ye have, and give alms; provide yourselves bags which wax not old, a treasure in the heavens that faileth not, where no thief approacheth, neither moth corrupteth.

LUKE 22:32 - But I have prayed for thee, that thy faith fail not: and when thou art converted, strengthen thy brethren.

1 CORINTHIANS 13:8 - Charity never faileth: but whether there be prophecies, they shall fail; whether there be tongues, they shall cease; whether there be knowledge, it shall vanish away.

3 JOHN 1:2 - Beloved, I wish above all things that thou mayest prosper and be in health, even as thy soul prospereth.

TEMPTATION

PSALMS 119:11 - Thy word have I hid in mine heart, that I might not sin against thee.

MATTHEW 26:41 - Watch and pray, that ye enter not into temptation: the spirit indeed is willing, but the flesh is weak.

ROMANS 6:14 - For sin shall not have dominion over you: for ye are not under the law, but under grace.

1 CORINTHIANS 6:18 - Flee fornication. Every sin that a man doeth is without the body; but he that committeth fornication sinneth against his own body.

1 CORINTHIANS 10:12-14 - Wherefore let him that thinketh he standeth take heed lest he fall. There hath no temptation taken you but such as is common to man: but God is faithful, who will not suffer you to be tempted above that ye are able; but will with the temptation also make a way to escape, that ye may be able to bear it. Wherefore, my dearly beloved, flee from idolatry.

2 CORINTHIANS 6:17-18 - Wherefore come out from among them, and be ye separate, saith the Lord, and touch not the unclean thing; and I will receive you, And will be a Father unto you, and ye shall be my sons and daughters, saith the Lord Almighty.

GALATIANS 5:16 - This I say then, Walk in the Spirit, and ye shall not fulfil the lust of the flesh.

GALATIANS 6:1-2 - Brethren, if a man be overtaken in a fault, ye which are spiritual, restore such an one in the spirit of meekness; considering thyself, lest thou also be tempted. Bear ye one another's burdens, and so fulfil the law of Christ.

EPHESIANS 6:10-11 - Finally, my brethren, be strong in the Lord, and in the power of his might. Put on the whole armour of God, that ye may be able to stand against the wiles of the devil.

1 TIMOTHY 6:9-11 - But they that will be rich fall into temptation and a snare, and into many foolish and hurtful lusts, which drown men in destruction and perdition. For the love of money is the root of all evil: which while some coveted after, they have erred from the faith, and pierced themselves through with many sorrows. But thou, O man of God, flee these things; and follow after righteousness, godliness, faith, love, patience, meekness.

2 TIMOTHY 2:22 - Flee also youthful lusts: but follow righteousness, faith, charity, peace, with them that call on the Lord out of a pure heart.

HEBREWS 2:18 - For in that he himself hath suffered being tempted, he is able to succour them that are tempted.

HEBREWS 4:15-16 - For we have not an high priest which cannot be touched with the feeling of our infirmities; but was in all points tempted like as we are, yet without sin. Let us therefore come boldly unto the throne of grace, that we may obtain mercy, and find grace to help in time of need.

JAMES 1:2-4 - My brethren, count it all joy when ye fall into divers temptations; Knowing this, that the trying of your faith worketh patience. But let patience have her perfect work, that ye may be perfect and entire, wanting nothing.

JAMES 1:12 - Blessed is the man that endureth temptation: for when he is tried, he shall receive the crown of life, which the Lord hath promised to them that love him.

JAMES 1:13-15 - Let no man say when he is tempted, I am tempted of God: for God cannot be tempted with evil, neither tempteth he any man: But every man is tempted, when he is drawn away of his own lust, and enticed. Then when lust hath conceived, it bringeth forth sin: and sin, when it is finished, bringeth forth death.

JAMES 4:7 - Submit yourselves therefore to God. Resist the devil, and he will flee from you.

1 PETER 1:6-7 - Wherein ye greatly rejoice, though now for a season, if need be, ye are in heaviness through manifold temptations: That the trial of your faith, being much more precious than of gold that perisheth, though it be tried with fire, might be found unto praise and honour and glory at the appearing of Jesus Christ:

1 PETER 4:12-13 - Beloved, think it not strange concerning the fiery trial which is to try you, as though some strange thing happened unto you: But rejoice, inasmuch as ye are partakers of Christ's sufferings; that, when his glory shall be revealed, ye may be glad also with exceeding joy.

1 PETER 5:8-9 - Be sober, be vigilant; because your adversary the devil, as a roaring lion, walketh about, seeking whom he may devour: Whom resist stedfast in the faith, knowing that the same afflictions are accomplished in your brethren that are in the world.

2 PETER 2:9 - The Lord knoweth how to deliver the godly out of temptations, and to reserve the unjust unto the day of judgment to be punished:

1 JOHN 1:9 - If we confess our sins, he is faithful and just to forgive us our sins, and to cleanse us from all unrighteousness.

1 JOHN 5:18 - We know that whosoever is born of God sinneth not; but he that is begotten of God keepeth himself, and that wicked one toucheth him not.

JUDE 1:24 - Now unto him that is able to keep you from falling, and to present you faultless before the presence of his glory with exceeding joy,

TRIALS & TRIBULATIONS

2 SAMUEL 22:18-19 - He delivered me from my strong enemy, and from them that hated me: for they were too strong for me. They prevented me in the day of my calamity: but the LORD was my stay.

2 SAMUEL 22:48-49 - It is God that avengeth me, and that bringeth down the people under me, And that bringeth me forth from mine enemies: thou also hast lifted me up on high above them that rose up against me: thou hast delivered me from the violent man.

2 KINGS 17:39 - But the LORD your God ye shall fear; and he shall deliver you out of the hand of all your enemies.

PSALMS 34:6 - This poor man cried, and the LORD heard him, and saved him out of all his troubles.

PSALMS 34:17 - The righteous cry, and the LORD heareth, and delivereth them out of all their troubles.

PSALMS 37:1 - Fret not thyself because of evildoers, neither be thou envious against the workers of iniquity.

PSALMS 37:18-19 - The LORD knoweth the days of the upright: and their inheritance shall be for ever. They shall not be ashamed in the evil time: and in the days of famine they shall be satisfied.

PSALMS 41:1 - Blessed is he that considereth the poor: the LORD will deliver him in time of trouble.

PSALMS 46:1 - God is our refuge and strength, a very present help in trouble.

PSALMS 50:14-15 - Offer unto God thanksgiving; and pay thy vows unto the most High: And call upon me in the day of trouble: I will deliver thee, and thou shalt glorify me.

PSALMS 54:7 - For he hath delivered me out of all trouble: and mine eye hath seen his desire upon mine enemies.

PSALMS 60:11 - Give us help from trouble: for vain is the help of man.

PSALMS 86:7 - In the day of my trouble I will call upon thee: for thou wilt answer me.

PSALMS 94:12-13 - Blessed is the man whom thou chastenest, O LORD, and teachest him out of thy law; That thou mayest give him rest from the days of adversity, until the pit be digged for the wicked.

PSALMS 107:6 - Then they cried unto the LORD in their trouble, and he delivered them out of their distresses.

PSALMS 138:7 - Though I walk in the midst of trouble, thou wilt revive me: thou shalt stretch forth thine hand against the wrath of mine enemies, and thy right hand shall save me.

PROVERBS 11:8 - The righteous is delivered out of trouble, and the wicked cometh in his stead.

PROVERBS 12:13 - The wicked is snared by the transgression of his lips: but the just shall come out of trouble.

PROVERBS 12:21 - There shall no evil happen to the just: but the wicked shall be filled with mischief.

PROVERBS 19:23 - The fear of the LORD tendeth to life: and he that hath it shall abide satisfied; he shall not be visited with evil.

ISAIAH 41:10 - Fear thou not; for I am with thee: be not dismayed; for I am thy God: I will strengthen thee; yea, I will help thee; yea, I will uphold thee with the right hand of my righteousness.

ISAIAH 54:14-15 - In righteousness shalt thou be established: thou shalt be far from oppression; for thou shalt not fear: and from terror; for it shall not come near thee. Behold, they shall surely gather together, but not by me: whosoever shall gather together against thee shall fall for thy sake.

2 CORINTHIANS 2:14 - Now thanks be unto God, which always causeth us to triumph in Christ, and maketh manifest the savour of his knowledge by us in every place.

2 THESSALONIANS 3:3 - But the Lord is faithful, who shall stablish you, and keep you from evil.

2 TIMOTHY 3:10-11 - But thou hast fully known my doctrine, manner of life, purpose, faith, longsuffering, charity, patience, persecutions, afflictions, which came unto me at Antioch, at Iconium, at Lystra; what persecutions I endured: but out of them all the Lord delivered me.

1 PETER 3:13 - And who is he that will harm you, if ye be followers of that which is good?

VICTORY

PSALMS 60:12 - Through God we shall do valiantly: for he it is that shall tread down our enemies.

PSALMS 92:4 - For thou, LORD, hast made me glad through thy work: I will triumph in the works of thy hands.

JOHN 16:33 - These things I have spoken unto you, that in me ye might have peace. In the world ye shall have tribulation: but be of good cheer; I have overcome the world.

ACTS 19:20 - So mightily grew the word of God and prevailed.

ROMANS 8:2 - For the law of the Spirit of life in Christ Jesus hath made me free from the law of sin and death.

ROMANS 8:31 - What shall we then say to these things? If God be for us, who can be against us?

ROMANS 8:37 - Nay, in all these things we are more than conquerors through him that loved us.

ROMANS 12:21 - Be not overcome of evil, but overcome evil with good.

1 CORINTHIANS 15:57 - But thanks be to God, which giveth us the victory through our Lord Jesus Christ.

2 CORINTHIANS 2:14 - Now thanks be unto God, which always causeth us to triumph in Christ, and maketh manifest the savour of his knowledge by us in every place.

EPHESIANS 6:10 - Finally, my brethren, be strong in the Lord, and in the power of his might.

PHILIPPIANS 4:13 - I can do all things through Christ which strengtheneth me.

1 JOHN 2:13 - I write unto you, fathers, because ye have known him that is from the beginning. I write unto you, young men, because ye have overcome the wicked one. I write unto you, little children, because ye have known the Father.

1 JOHN 4:4 - Ye are of God, little children, and have overcome them: because greater is he that is in you, than he that is in the world.

1 JOHN 5:4 - For whatsoever is born of God overcometh the world: and this is the victory that overcometh the world, even our faith.

REVELATION 2:17 - He that hath an ear, let him hear what the Spirit saith unto the churches; To him that overcometh will I give to eat of the hidden manna, and will give him a white stone, and in the stone a new name written, which no man knoweth saving he that receiveth it.

REVELATION 2:26-28 - And he that overcometh, and keepeth my works unto the end, to him will I give power over the nations: And he shall rule them with a rod of iron; as the vessels of a potter shall they be broken to shivers: even as I received of my Father. And I will give him the morning star.

REVELATION 3:5 - He that overcometh, the same shall be clothed in white raiment; and I will not blot out his name out of the book of life, but I will confess his name before my Father, and before his angels.

REVELATION 3:12 - Him that overcometh will I make a pillar in the temple of my God, and he shall go no more out: and I will write upon him the name of my God, and the name of the city of my God, which is new Jerusalem, which cometh down out of heaven from my God: and I will write upon him my new name.

REVELATION 3:21 - To him that overcometh will I grant to sit with me in my throne, even as I also overcame, and am set down with my Father in his throne.

REVELATION 12:11 - And they overcame him by the blood of the Lamb, and by the word of their testimony; and they loved not their lives unto the death.

REVELATION 21:7 - He that overcometh shall inherit all things; and I will be his God, and he shall be my son.

WISDOM

DEUTERONOMY 4:5-6 - Behold, I have taught you statutes and judgments, even as the LORD my God commanded me, that ye should do so in the land whither ye go to possess it. Keep therefore and do them; for this is your wisdom and your understanding in the sight of the nations, which shall hear all these statutes, and say, Surely this great nation is a wise and understanding people.

DEUTERONOMY 16:19 - Thou shalt not wrest judgment; thou shalt not respect persons, neither take a gift: for a gift doth blind the eyes of the wise, and pervert the words of the righteous.

1 KINGS 3:28 - And all Israel heard of the judgment which the king had judged; and they feared the king: for they saw that the wisdom of God was in him, to do judgment.

2 CHRONICLES 1:10 - Give me now wisdom and knowledge, that I may go out and come in before this people: for who can judge this thy people, that is so great?

JOB 28:28 - And unto man he said, Behold, the fear of the Lord, that is wisdom; and to depart from evil is understanding.

JOB 32:9 - Great men are not always wise: neither do the aged understand judgment.

PSALMS 19:7 - The law of the LORD is perfect, converting the soul: the testimony of the LORD is sure, making wise the simple.

PSALMS 37:30 - The mouth of the righteous speaketh wisdom, and his tongue talketh of judgment.

PSALMS 49:3 - My mouth shall speak of wisdom; and the meditation of my heart shall be of understanding.

PSALMS 51:6 - Behold, thou desirest truth in the inward parts: and in the hidden part thou shalt make me to know wisdom.

PSALMS 101:2 - I will behave myself wisely in a perfect way. O when wilt thou come unto me? I will walk within my house with a perfect heart.

PSALMS 107:43 - Whoso is wise, and will observe these things, even they shall understand the lovingkindness of the LORD.

PSALMS 111:10 - The fear of the LORD is the beginning of wisdom: a good understanding have all they that do his commandments: his praise endureth for ever.

PSALMS 119:98 - Thou through thy commandments hast made me wiser than mine enemies: for they are ever with me.

PROVERBS 1:5 - A wise man will hear, and will increase learning; and a man of understanding shall attain unto wise counsels:

PROVERBS 1:20,33 - Wisdom crieth without; she uttereth her voice in the streets: But whoso hearkeneth unto me shall dwell safely, and shall be quiet from fear of evil.

PROVERBS 2:6 - For the LORD giveth wisdom: out of his mouth cometh knowledge and understanding.

PROVERBS 3:7 - Be not wise in thine own eyes: fear the LORD, and depart from evil.

PROVERBS 3:13,16-17 - Happy is the man that findeth wisdom, and the man that getteth understanding. Length of days is in her right hand; and in her left hand riches and honour. Her ways are ways of pleasantness, and all her paths are peace.

PROVERBS 3:35 - The wise shall inherit glory: but shame shall be the promotion of fools.

PROVERBS 4:5-8 - Get wisdom, get understanding: forget it not; neither decline from the words of my mouth. Forsake her not, and she shall preserve thee: love her, and she shall keep thee. Wisdom is the principal thing; therefore get wisdom: and with all thy getting get understanding. Exalt her, and she shall promote thee: she shall bring thee to honour, when thou dost embrace her.

PROVERBS 8:12,21 - I wisdom dwell with prudence, and find out knowledge of witty inventions. That I may cause those that love me to inherit substance; and I will fill their treasures.

PROVERBS 8:33 - Hear instruction, and be wise, and refuse it not.

PROVERBS 9:1 - Wisdom hath builded her house, she hath hewn out her seven pillars:

PROVERBS 9:9 - Give instruction to a wise man, and he will be yet wiser: teach a just man, and he will increase in learning.

PROVERBS 10:1 - A wise son maketh a glad father: but a foolish son is the heaviness of his mother.

PROVERBS 10:5 - He that gathereth in summer is a wise son: but he that sleepeth in harvest is a son that causeth shame.

PROVERBS 10:8 - The wise in heart will receive commandments: but a prating fool shall fall.

PROVERBS 10:13-14 - In the lips of him that hath understanding wisdom is found: but a rod is for the back of him that is void of understanding. Wise men lay up knowledge: but the mouth of the foolish is near destruction.

PROVERBS 10:14 - Wise men lay up knowledge: but the mouth of the foolish is near destruction.

PROVERBS 11:2 - When pride cometh, then cometh shame: but with the lowly is wisdom.

PROVERBS 11:30 - The fruit of the righteous is a tree of life; and he that winneth souls is wise.

PROVERBS 12:15 - The way of a fool is right in his own eyes: but he that hearkeneth unto counsel is wise.

PROVERBS 12:18 - There is that speaketh like the piercings of a sword: but the tongue of the wise is health.

PROVERBS 13:1 - A wise son heareth his father's instruction: but a scorner heareth not rebuke.

PROVERBS 13:10 - Only by pride cometh contention: but with the well advised is wisdom.

PROVERBS 13:20 - He that walketh with wise men shall be wise: but a companion of fools shall be destroyed.

PROVERBS 14:3 - In the mouth of the foolish is a rod of pride: but the lips of the wise shall preserve them.

PROVERBS 14:33 - Wisdom resteth in the heart of him that hath understanding: but that which is in the midst of fools is made known.

PROVERBS 15:2 - The tongue of the wise useth knowledge aright: but the mouth of fools poureth out foolishness.

PROVERBS 15:7 - The lips of the wise disperse knowledge: but the heart of the foolish doeth not so.

PROVERBS 15:24 - The way of life is above to the wise, that he may depart from hell beneath.

PROVERBS 15:31 - The ear that heareth the reproof of life abideth among the wise.

PROVERBS 16:16 - How much better is it to get wisdom than gold! and to get understanding rather to be chosen than silver!

PROVERBS 16:20 - He that handleth a matter wisely shall find good: and whoso trusteth in the LORD, happy is he.

PROVERBS 16:23 - The heart of the wise teacheth his mouth, and addeth learning to his lips.

PROVERBS 17:2 - A wise servant shall have rule over a son that causeth shame, and shall have part of the inheritance among the brethren.

PROVERBS 17:28 - Even a fool, when he holdeth his peace, is counted wise: and he that shutteth his lips is esteemed a man of understanding.

PROVERBS 18:15 - The heart of the prudent getteth knowledge; and the ear of the wise seeketh knowledge.

PROVERBS 19:20 - Hear counsel, and receive instruction, that thou mayest be wise in thy latter end.

PROVERBS 20:1 - Wine is a mocker, strong drink is raging: and whosoever is deceived thereby is not wise.

PROVERBS 21:11 - When the scorner is punished, the simple is made wise: and when the wise is instructed, he receiveth knowledge.

PROVERBS 21:22 - A wise man scaleth the city of the mighty, and casteth down the strength of the confidence thereof.

PROVERBS 23:19 - Hear thou, my son, and be wise, and guide thine heart in the way.

PROVERBS 24:3 - Through wisdom is an house builded; and by understanding it is established:

PROVERBS 24:5-6 - A wise man is strong; yea, a man of knowledge increaseth strength. For by wise counsel thou shalt make thy war: and in multitude of counsellors there is safety.

PROVERBS 25:12 - As an earring of gold, and an ornament of fine gold, so is a wise reprover upon an obedient ear.

PROVERBS 28:7 - Whoso keepeth the law is a wise son: but he that is a companion of riotous men shameth his father.

PROVERBS 28:26 - He that trusteth in his own heart is a fool: but whoso walketh wisely, he shall be delivered.

PROVERBS 29:8 - Scornful men bring a city into a snare: but wise men turn away wrath.

PROVERBS 29:15 - The rod and reproof give wisdom: but a child left to himself bringeth his mother to shame.

ECCLESIASTES 4:13 - Better is a poor and a wise child than an old and foolish king, who will no more be admonished.

ECCLESIASTES 7:5 - It is better to hear the rebuke of the wise, than for a man to hear the song of fools.

ECCLESIASTES 7:7 - Surely oppression maketh a wise man mad; and a gift destroyeth the heart.

ECCLESIASTES 7:11-12 - Wisdom is good with an inheritance: and by it there is profit to them that see the sun. For wisdom is a defence, and money is a defence: but the excellency of knowledge is, that wisdom giveth life to them that have it.

ECCLESIASTES 7:19 - Wisdom strengtheneth the wise more than ten mighty men which are in the city.

ECCLESIASTES 8:1 - Who is as the wise man? and who knoweth the interpretation of a thing? a man's wisdom maketh his face to shine, and the boldness of his face shall be changed.

ECCLESIASTES 8:5 - Whoso keepeth the commandment shall feel no evil thing: and a wise man's heart discerneth both time and judgment.

ECCLESIASTES 9:16 - Then said I, Wisdom is better than strength: nevertheless the poor man's wisdom is despised, and his words are not heard.

ECCLESIASTES 9:18 - Wisdom is better than weapons of war: but one sinner destroyeth much good.

ECCLESIASTES 10:10 - If the iron be blunt, and he do not whet the edge, then must he put to more strength: but wisdom is profitable to direct.

DANIEL 2:20-21 - Daniel answered and said, Blessed be the name of God for ever and ever: for wisdom and might are his: And he changeth the times and the seasons: he removeth kings, and setteth up kings: he giveth wisdom unto the wise, and knowledge to them that know understanding:

DANIEL 12:10 - Many shall be purified, and made white, and tried; but the wicked shall do wickedly: and none of the wicked shall understand; but the wise shall understand.

MATTHEW 7:24 - Therefore whosoever heareth these sayings of mine, and doeth them, I will liken him unto a wise man, which built his house upon a rock:

MATTHEW 11:19 - The Son of man came eating and drinking, and they say, Behold a man gluttonous, and a winebibber, a friend of publicans and sinners. But wisdom is justified of her children.

LUKE 2:40,52 - And the child grew, and waxed strong in spirit, filled with wisdom: and the grace of God was upon him. And Jesus increased in wisdom and stature, and in favour with God and man.

LUKE 21:15 - For I will give you a mouth and wisdom, which all your adversaries shall not be able to gainsay nor resist.

ACTS 6:3 - Wherefore, brethren, look ye out among you seven men of honest report, full of the Holy Ghost and wisdom, whom we may appoint over this business.

ACTS 6:10 - And they were not able to resist the wisdom and the spirit by which he spake.

ROMANS 11:33 - O the depth of the riches both of the wisdom and knowledge of God! how unsearchable are his judgments, and his ways past finding out!

ROMANS 16:19 - For your obedience is come abroad unto all men. I am glad therefore on your behalf: but yet I would have you wise unto that which is good, and simple concerning evil.

1 CORINTHIANS 1:24-25 - But unto them which are called, both Jews and Greeks, Christ the power of God, and the wisdom of God. Because the foolishness of God is wiser than men; and the weakness of God is stronger than men.

1 CORINTHIANS 1:30 - But of him are ye in Christ Jesus, who of God is made unto us wisdom, and righteousness, and sanctification, and redemption:

1 CORINTHIANS 4:10 - We are fools for Christ's sake, but ye are wise in Christ; we are weak, but ye are strong; ye are honourable, but we are despised.

EPHESIANS 1:8 - Wherein he hath abounded toward us in all wisdom and prudence;

EPHESIANS 1:17 - That the God of our Lord Jesus Christ, the Father of glory, may give unto you the spirit of wisdom and revelation in the knowledge of him:

EPHESIANS 3:10 - To the intent that now unto the principalities and powers in heavenly places might be known by the church the manifold wisdom of God,

PHILIPPIANS 2:5 - Let this mind be in you, which was also in Christ Jesus:

COLOSSIANS 1:9 - For this cause we also, since the day we heard it, do not cease to pray for you, and to desire that ye might be filled with the knowledge of his will in all wisdom and spiritual understanding;

COLOSSIANS 2:2-3 - That their hearts might be comforted, being knit together in love, and unto all riches of the full assurance of understanding, to the acknowledgment of the mystery of God, and of the Father, and of Christ; In whom are hid all the treasures of wisdom and knowledge.

COLOSSIANS 3:16 - Let the word of Christ dwell in you richly in all wisdom; teaching and admonishing one another in psalms and hymns and spiritual songs, singing with grace in your hearts to the Lord.

1 TIMOTHY 1:17 - Now unto the King eternal, immortal, invisible, the only wise God, be honour and glory for ever and ever. Amen.

2 TIMOTHY 3:15 - And that from a child thou hast known the holy scriptures, which are able to make thee wise unto salvation through faith which is in Christ Jesus.

JAMES 1:5 - If any of you lack wisdom, let him ask of God, that giveth to all men liberally, and upbraideth not; and it shall be given him.

JAMES 3:13 - Who is a wise man and endued with knowledge among you? let him show out of a good conversation his works with meekness of wisdom.

JAMES 3:17 - But the wisdom that is from above is first pure, then peaceable, gentle, and easy to be entreated, full of mercy and good fruits, without partiality, and without hypocrisy.

YOUR HEALING
DOOR

12 KEYS THAT CAN UNLOCK HEALING FOR YOU AND THOSE YOU LOVE

To order your copy of Greg Mohr's book on healing please visit www.yourhealingdoor.com

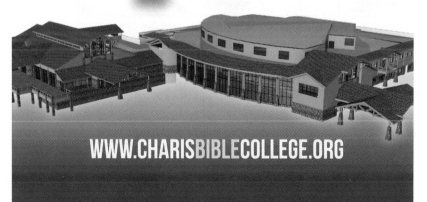